Aid and self-help

Aid and self-help

A GENERAL GUIDE TO OVERSEAS AID

ELIZABETH O'KELLY

CHARLES KNIGHT & CO LTD 1973
LONDON & TONBRIDGE

911.302

Charles Knight & Co. Ltd.
11-12 Bury Street, London, EC3A 5AP
Dowgate Works, Douglas Road, Tonbridge
Copyright © 1973 Elizabeth O'Kelly
Filmset and printed in Great Britain by
BAS Printers Limited, Wallop, Hampshire

ISBN 0 85314 167 3

Contents

List of illustrations

Preface

Whenever a disaster occurs, man-made or natural, the world
rushes to the rescue, but too often the result is almost as
disastrous as the disaster itself. The immense sum of money
raised after the Aberfan landslide in Britain, for example,
may have helped to alleviate the sufferings of some of the
victims but it has sadly disrupted the life of the community.
Similarly much of the aid poured into Biafra and India, at
the time of the Bangladesh crisis, by the manner of its
giving so alienated the governments concerned as to hinder
rather than help the very people it set out to assist.

Throughout the world there is an enormous fund of good-
will often dispensed with very little knowledge of conditions
in the country to which aid is being sent. Television programmes and newspaper reports tend to dwell on the horrors
of the disaster itself and say little about the efforts being
made to put matters right. Part One of this book therefore
attempts to distinguish between the varying types of refugees,
with their differing needs, and makes suggestions as to how
best to meet these by making use, whenever possible, of
local resources.

Overseas aid, however, is not confined to disasters. The
United Nations Organisation and most Western countries
have aid programmes in both Africa and Asia and it is this
type of assistance which is discussed in Part Two with
particular reference to rural development schemes and with
the emphasis on self help whenever practicable. Part Three
describes how one such programme was successfully carried

out in the Cameroons.

It is hoped that this book may be of use to people planning to take part in rural development work overseas and may persuade them and the organisations which send them to encourage the people of the developing countries to take a more active part in projects for their own welfare than they are always permitted to do at present.

If it also helps the man in the street to understand better the problems of the rural people in the Third World and their customs, it will have served an additional purpose.

I The various types of disaster

We live in a time of disaster. One follows the other in swift succession—or so it would seem, but whether, in fact, this is indeed the case or whether it is merely that, through improved communications, we now hear almost immediately of events of which we might never have known in the past is a matter for speculation.

It is, however, an unfortunate fact that this very ease of communication, and especially travel, has not brought about a better understanding between nations. Rather the contrary —and technological advances which are often so spectacularly employed when a disaster strikes are themselves sometimes responsible for it by destroying the balance of nature.

Two world wars have cheapened the value of human life and, although the conscience of the world can still be stirred when there is any very great human suffering, the aid given, by the way it is given, sometimes aggravates what it sets out to alleviate. Through television programmes, of sometimes doubtful accuracy, the man in the street is now familiar with persons and places formerly known only to experienced travellers. But unfortunately far from increasing our knowledge and appreciation of their customs and culture, the effect is to reduce everything to the same rather dreary common factor.

Because tropical areas are more liable to earthquakes, cyclones and flooding, natural disasters tend to occur most often in developing countries whose economy is the least

1

able to bear them. When they strike elsewhere, as for example in Alaska, the country is better fitted to cope with them and any help sent from outside is due more to a desire on the part of other nations to show their sympathy than because it is a necessity. It is for this reason, therefore, that this book deals mostly with the effects of disaster in Africa and Asia, since it is in these areas that disasters have the greatest impact economically. The term "developing" should not necessarily be equated with "backward", for many countries so designated have a history and culture equal to any in the West. The definition relates to their economic standing and is based on the average income *per capita*.

Whenever a disaster occurs, basically the same routine is put into operation by the would-be helpers, but the root cause of these disasters can differ very greatly and it is important to understand this if aid is to be fully effective.

In a "man-made" disaster, such as the fighting in Nigeria, or the more recent events in East Pakistan, now Bangladesh, which have led to one of the biggest movements of population in the history of the world, the whole situation will be confused by emotional undertones politically inspired. Each side will issue totally different versions of the same incident, whilst many of the helpers from overseas will be equally partisan. Victims will exaggerate their sufferings in order to gain more support for their cause, stories of atrocities and mismanagement will abound and both sides will do their best to prevent aid from reaching the other.

In a natural disaster, however, such as the three bad earthquakes in Turkey in recent years, the situation will be quite different. Once communications have been restored and it is possible to get to the scene of the disaster, it will be possible to assess the situation objectively and all people and all countries will be willing to join together in the relief work. Unlike "man-made" disasters, these natural disasters make little distinction between rich and poor. All are likely to suffer equally, but in a disaster of a political nature the rich have often been forewarned and usually have the means to escape, and the poor are probably the principal sufferers.

The rural population, moreover, often suffer more than the town dwellers to whom numbers give a certain security.

It has been said that this century will be known in later years as the age of the refugee, and the truth of this is becoming increasingly apparent. Refugees, however, fall into a number of different categories. Failure to appreciate this means that they are often all treated in the same way, and before aid can be really effective it is first necessary to establish into which category they come.

In the first category might be said to be those who are victims of war and these again can be divided into three more groups. The first covers those who have actually been bombed, burned or otherwise driven out of their homes. They will usually have lost everything, and will probably be injured and humiliated as well as frightened. They will certainly be in a state of shock and quite possibly separated from other members of their family, with all its attendant anxieties. Their morale will be low and their need for help immediate. The other two groups in this category, however, are more properly called displaced persons than refugees. Some will possibly have been moved from their homes for reasons of security—the army, for example, may be planning a drive in their area (this type of displacement was very common in South Viet-Nam before large-scale military operations). These people will probably have been able to bring their more portable possessions with them, may even have been brought to the refugee camp in army lorries, and may well be able to return to their homes again as soon as the operation is completed. Meanwhile, they will be lodged in different types of temporary accommodation, such as refugee camps and villages, and shanty towns which may spring up very rapidly. In urban areas, schools are sometimes taken over to house refugees.

But the third group in this first category, although they, too, may have been able to bring their belongings with them, may be moving into permanent exile, for example, the Arab refugees in the Middle East who appear to have little hope of ever being able to return to their former homes, or the

3

1   Urban refugees camping out in a large school in Saigon. In the foreground is the type of oil stove which can be purchased inexpensively in most Asian countries. It has the advantage of enabling refugees to cook for themselves.

persons who migrated during the time of the partition of India, to say nothing of the immense numbers of stateless persons displaced by the Second World War. The physical sufferings of these unfortunate beings may be less than that of the refugees in the first groups but their morale will be the lowest. A few may be able to make a new start but the majority, like persons prematurely retired, will lapse into inertia, lacking the will to help themselves and proving, in the long run, by far the most difficult group to deal with.

These were all in the first category—the victims of war; into the second come the victims of natural disasters. They, too, may be injured and also shocked and may be separated from their families; but, since the flooding or the earthquake or whatever has caused the disaster cannot go on for ever, they can see an end to their sufferings. Undivided by political differences they will probably be more willing to help each other. With help from others, they will begin the reconstruction of their homes as soon as it is safe to do so, probably on exactly the same spot as before despite the possibility of a repetition of the disaster at some later date. Although actual conditions at first may be the most chaotic, these will be the refugees whom it will prove easiest to help in the end.

II The contribution made by non-governmental organisations

Once a disaster strikes the various relief organisations throughout the world, together with their governments, move into action. Unfortunately it is too frequently forgotten that the government of the country in which the disaster has occurred still exists and will have its own views on how to deal with the situation and whether, in fact, it wants (which is different from needs) aid from outside at all. If it is a "man-made" disaster, this government will be chary of accepting anything which may seem to it to have "strings" attached to it, or of agreeing to anything which might be taken as an indication that it was not fully in control of the situation. If it is a natural disaster, the government may feel that it is better qualified to deal with the emergency than its would-be helpers, since it is probably by no means the first time such an event has occurred there. What it probably lacks, if it is a developing country, is not the "know how", but the financial means to carry out the rescue work—helicopters and bulldozers cost money.

In these circumstances, and this has occurred in almost all the recent disasters affecting developing countries, a situation develops in which the world rushes to assist. It is then surprised that it is rebuffed by the local government whose dignity is affronted, or who is suspicious of their motives; and a good deal of the blame for this state of affairs must lie with the West, which does not always take national pride sufficiently into account.

The all too familiar stories then follow in the Western

6

press of aid materials rotting on the wharves because of official red tape, and of overseas personnel being asked to leave almost as soon as they have arrived, if indeed, they are admitted at all. The fact that this state of affairs is sometimes due to the people concerned having taken advantage of the chaos to by-pass entry regulations is not always referred to. Nor is it always remembered that, everywhere, in time of war, spy scares abound, whilst the off-beat, well-intentioned but essentially muddle-headed idealists (which occasions like this always seem to attract) who insist on forcing their way in, in the name of humanity, or personal freedom, only succeed in making things much more difficult for everyone else. In South Viet-Nam the work of all the refugee organisations there was imperilled, and much more stringent conditions were imposed upon them, because of some journalists who disappeared into the interior in search of copy in violation of their entry permits.

It is not unknown for Customs officials everywhere to be difficult if documents are not in order and the East does not have a monopoly in this sort of thing (the Babu mentality is, after all the product of the old British-trained Indian Civil service). It takes initiative to cut across regulations, and junior officials are not encouraged to exercise this. It is, therefore, pointless to shout and storm at them, which will only produce a rocklike resistance and damage relationships for the future. The remedy is surely to see that the goods are consigned correctly in the first place, which is not always the case now.

When a disaster strikes there are many relief organisations able and willing to come to the rescue. One of the foremost is the International Red Cross Committee which, as the world has good cause to remember, has a splendid record in disaster relief. Troubles have unfortunately arisen between it and local governments in recent years, notably in Nigeria at the time of the civil war. A reason for this may be that this Committee is not, as is sometimes believed, the co-ordinating body of the National Red Cross Societies—this is the League of Red Cross Societies—and as more and more

7

B

developing countries set up their own National Societies, these increasingly feel that they themselves, rather than the International Committee, are capable of handling any disaster which may occur in their own country. This difficulty is perhaps accentuated by the fact that, whilst Switzerland has a humanitarian record second to none, for reasons of history it has had less experience than some others in dealing with newly independent nations. It is possible, therefore that the Swiss businessmen, who largely make up the Committee, perhaps fail to take national feelings sufficiently into account in their negotiations, whilst the governments with whom they are dealing in their turn fail to recognise their excellent intentions.

In the case of most of the other international voluntary organisations working in this field, they are often better fitted to deal with the long-term aspects of a disaster than with the immediate relief work, which if it is very complex, may be beyond their financial and technical resources. In addition, although those who are connected with Christian Missions overseas may be genuinely activated by humanitarian considerations alone, in non-Christian countries the governments are unlikely entirely to believe this and will fear attempts at conversion. Even in normal times, it is now difficult for clergymen to visit India unless they are described only as "social workers" on their passports.

These voluntary organisations usually have one enormous advantage over Governments, however, in that they can often draw upon their local workers on the spot for an assessment of the situation and can use them as the spearhead of their efforts. This may not, however, be true if the disaster is due to civil war. Then these assistants, mindful of their position when the war ends, will be anxious to avoid involvement as much as possible for fear of later reprisals. This is one of the reasons why it is usually much easier to find local helpers in the event of a natural disaster than when a political one is involved.

One further point needs to be taken into consideration, too, when assessing the part these organisations can play in relief work. They are supported by voluntary funds and ultimately will have to justify both their actions and their expenditure to their supporters. Should they fail to do so to their satisfaction, their funds may dry up. This sometimes causes them to cry havoc more loudly than events perhaps merit and can also lead to a certain rivalry between them which, whilst understandable, is not desirable. This state of affairs was regrettably obvious in South Viet-Nam where practically every major international relief organisation was represented and where almost every incident led to fierce competition to take over the relief work, despite the fact that the Government of Viet-Nam had already set up its own Ministry for Refugees and needed material assistance rather than advice.

A welcome step in the right direction, however, has been taken in Britain where the Voluntary Committee on Overseas Aid and Development has been formed by eight of the major relief organisations to ensure the co-ordination of their overseas programmes and a similar organisation now exists in the United States.

When one considers the type of volunteer sent out to take part in relief work by most of these organisations, the youth of many of the volunteers is something of a disadvantage, though one must admit that it is difficult to avoid. Men and women in their thirties, who would be more suitable, are established in their careers by that age and unable, or unwilling, to abandon them for short-term rescue operations. This is particularly true of doctors. Some countries allow medical volunteers credit for their overseas service, which must be valuable experience for them, but this is not the case in Britain, although such a course should be strongly advocated.

But most young volunteers, however dedicated—and many of them undoubtedly are—are unlikely to have the background knowledge which is essential if their work is to be immediately effective, unless they are students of anthropology or sociology, in which case their studies will have given them an insight into the problems of developing countries. They will not yet have had much opportunity to

9

widen their outlook by travel, they will lack judgement and they will still be at the age when they think that their way of doing something is the only one for, contrary to popular belief, we usually become more adaptable with age. For them it is all an adventure, and one from which they know they will be pulled out if things become impossible. For the refugees it is a grim reality from which there is little escape.

This is not to denigrate youth or to fail to recognise that their freshness of approach will have value but, in the early stages of a disaster when skill and experience are needed, it is doubtful whether they, or any other untrained workers who are able to contribute little more than another pair of hands, can replace the professionals who are really needed in these circumstances.

The part played by the U.N. High Commission for Refugees should not be overlooked in discussing contributions made to their welfare. Fridtjof Nansen was appointed the first High Commissioner as long ago as 1921, but the present office was established only in 1951 and has just celebrated its twentieth anniversary. It acts as liaison between governments and inter-governmental organisations and voluntary bodies and co-operates with the various other U.N. agencies. Inevitably this makes it somewhat unwieldy and it is not always able to get underway as rapidly as is desirable when an emergency occurs. Nevertheless, although not all the major governments yet contribute to its funds, it plays an important part in the permanent re-establishment of refugees, and is very much concerned with the present situation in India and Pakistan.

III The need for international and national relief corps

The question of assistance when a disaster strikes is one which is causing concern in a number of countries and organisations at present. The United Nations Organisation has recently appointed a Disaster Relief Co-ordinator who is stationed in Geneva. His role, at any rate for the time being, is largely an advisory one. In Britain five of the voluntary agencies concerned with overseas aid have established a Disaster Emergency Committee to co-ordinate their efforts, but as yet there is no permanent force whose sole task it is to help in time of disaster.

Relief work, however, can usually be divided into two stages, the first covering the immediate rescue operations, which may often be difficult and even dangerous, and the second concerned more with the actual welfare of the survivors, their re-housing, food and medical care, and the setting up of welfare services for them. The first stage is one in which the West can still play a valuable part by contributing its technical expertise, but it is becoming increasingly clear that the second is best left to the nationals of the country concerned.

The early days of an emergency call for quick thinking and skilled action by trained personnel operating highly complex equipment and such things as helicopters, launches and bulldozers which may not readily be available in the country in which the disaster has occurred. In the past, Western governments have often met such an emergency by sending in detachments from their armed services and by using their

11

air forces to fly goods in. Unfortunately this type of assistance is no longer always acceptable to the Third World. However *bona fide* their intentions, foreign troops entering a newly independent country will almost certainly give rise to accusations of political interference. On the other hand the world cannot simply stand by and do nothing faced with human suffering on the scale of that in East Pakistan at the time of the disastrous cyclone in 1970 or in Bengal in 1971, and it is clear, therefore, that some sort of *modus operandi* needs to be worked out which will be acceptable to all governments.

The one which would appear to be the most satisfactory for the first stage, and which is now being discussed in several quarters, is the setting up of a permanent international relief corps. Its members would be highly skilled technicians recruited from many countries, covering a wide range of experience. They would operate from a central headquarters, and be able to fly within a matter of hours to the scene of the disaster, taking all their machines and equipment with them and drawing relief supplies from a central stock pile established for that purpose.

A corps of this nature would almost certainly have to be initiated by and come under the United Nations Organisation. It would be essential for it to be placed directly under the command of the Secretary General himself to prevent the delays which might otherwise occur if it were attached to one of the U.N. Specialised Agencies whose constitutions often make it difficult for them to act quickly. Dr A. R. Michaelis in his *Disasters Past and Future* quotes figures compiled by the U.S. Department of State showing that from July 1st 1970 to June 30th 1971 there were 51 disasters affecting more than 68 million people in which over half a million people died. It is therefore, unfortunately, unlikely that an international corps would have to face long periods of inactivity but, should these occur, members could perhaps be used to give valuable technical advice to development projects overseas. The type of personnel required could probably be obtained most easily by secondment from the specialist branches of the armed services, but this time they would be serving under the United Nations' flag, not their national flag. Their conditions of service would presumably be similar to those in the U.N. peace-keeping force. Communications experts, civil engineers, sanitary and medical officers, and catering staff used to working with field kitchens would be the categories most likely to be needed, but civil defence workers might also have a useful contribution to make where buildings had collapsed because of an earthquake. The key role in the corps, however, would undoubtedly be that of the Supplies or Logistics officers, of whom there should be a number. They would need to be amongst the very first to fly out to the scene in order to send back reports as to the extent of the disaster and what exactly will be required in the way of assistance, as well as how much of this could be obtained by local purchase to relieve the pressure on communications. From the start they would need to liaise very closely with the government of the country concerned. The success of the whole operation might well depend on this, since it is the neglect of this courtesy which has often contributed to the difficulties with local officials which have arisen in past disasters, especially in respect of the consignment of goods from overseas.

But even if this international corps can be successfully established, it is not the complete answer to a disaster situation. Stage 2 has still to be faced.

In times of crisis, one of the greatest needs felt by the survivors is that of communication. Doctors and nurses cannot diagnose a patient's illness easily if they must work always through an interpreter, social workers who are unfamiliar with local customs and do not speak the language can make serious mistakes and are of little comfort to the sufferer, and would-be helpers who do not themselves eat or know how to prepare the local foods have a limited value. This was clearly demonstrated during the troubles in Biafra when Sir John Hunt, who was investigating the position there, received a very bad press when he ventured to say that he had not found food as scarce as had been made out. One suspects that his critics failed to recognise that yams and cassava were growing all round them, but were thinking in terms of Western foods. Africans themselves would not make this mistake.

Doctors in developing countries will often know of local medicines which may be more readily available in the circumstances than the one on which their Western colleagues have come to rely. They will be more used to working with improvised equipment and in poor conditions. If sometimes they appear not to handle problems as urgently as outsiders think desirable, it is often because experience has taught them that, in their climatic conditions, if they are to survive it is best to hasten slowly. They are far less often taken in by the malingerer who is queueing for medicines with the intention of selling them in the market, and they soon recognise the professional beggar who exists even in refugee camps. In short, they understand their own people far better than any outsider can do unless he has lived for years in the country.

Whilst, therefore, the international corps can play an invaluable part in the early days when the country concerned is still too shattered to help itself, after the initial shock has worn off and the first rescue operations completed, there is an excellent case for the withdrawal of the international corps in favour of a locally raised national corps made up of volunteers from the country itself. If this is universally agreed, the United Nations Organisation would again appear to be the best body to set the ball rolling by asking its member countries to set up registers of qualified volunteers able and willing to be called up in the event of a disaster striking their own country. Organisations somewhat on these lines are, of course, already in existence in some Western countries. To suggest that the developing countries might follow suit is a practicable proposition now that many of the doctors, nurses and social workers who have been sent overseas for training in recent years are back home again. Indeed, it might be said that the fact that this nucleus of trained workers has so often been overlooked in past rescue operations has possibly been a contributory cause to the tensions which have sometimes arisen between volunteers from outside and local workers.

Once volunteers had registered in the national corps they would continue with their normal employment, but might be expected to undertake, say, two weeks' training a year, the government making it obligatory on their employers to allow them the time off, with pay, and also to reinstate them in their former employment if it should prove necessary, in an emergency, to call them up for a longer period. The United Nations Organisation would see that basically the same training was carried out in all countries and the same equipment used, as far as possible, to make it easier for the international corps to link up with and eventually hand over to the local corps. Once the national corps had taken over, volunteers from overseas would work under its direction, and relief goods would be channelled through it, although, in this respect, it might be helpful if one of the international supplies officers remained behind after the international corps had left to ensure full co-ordination.

The cost of the international corps would presumably be met by the participating governments and by voluntary donations, and the cost of the national corps would be the concern of the country forming it. This two-tier structure should therefore not only ensure that future disasters could be dealt with more effectively than has been possible in the past, but also that the cost would be more evenly shared out. Whatever the pattern that develops, however, there can be no denying that a disaster relief plan is most urgently needed.

IV Material aid

It has often been reported, when an earthquake or cyclone or similar disaster has struck, that great difficulty has been encountered in getting relief to the victims because of the breakdown in communications. Yet very seldom does it appear than any attempt is made to overcome this problem by purchasing goods locally. This was illustrated when the U. N. High Commission for Refugees appealed to Western governments to help transport to Bengal some 5 million blankets it had purchased in America, Europe and Canada. Since the bulk of these appeared to be the type of cotton blanket which India itself manufactures one wonders why it was not possible to purchase at least some of them on the spot?

There are, of course, a variety of reasons why this is usually not done, and governments prefer to work through their embassies, and relief organisations to send in things from outside. The chief reason, although it is rarely expressed is, of course, the fear that any money sent may fall into wrong hands. This is indeed a possibility, one might even say probability, but the East and the West do not view these matters in the same light, and the real point at issue is the speed with which aid can be brought to the victims. It ought, perhaps, also to be remembered that the West itself is not entirely free from scandal in these matters. The newspapers have recently carried reports of an investigation into a suspected fraud involving relief supplies to both the East Pakistan flood disaster and Biafra, in which, it is alleged,

16

relief aid was used both as a cover for tax evasion and for profiteering by the selling of goods which were originally gifts. If, therefore, the local middleman *does* take his cut, when things are purchased in the country itself, it should also be realised that he will certainly purchase them more cheaply than a foreigner would be able to do, so that, in the end, things even out. Moreover, such a course of action would help to stimulate the local economy at a time when it may badly need this, and would probably mean that only medicines might have to be sent in from outside, since developing countries usually cannot afford to hold large stocks in tropical conditions, in which they deteriorate rapidly.

It is sad, but true, that much of the material aid sent out by the West, when a disaster strikes, is often unsuitable and sometimes unnecessary, and this applies especially to second-hand clothing. It can be doubted whether anyone really likes wearing other people's cast-offs, and to refugees they can be the final humiliation, especially in countries where they do not usually wear Western-type clothing.

In these cases, if they receive such garments, they will spend hours unpicking them to try to reshape them into something in which they will not stand out like a black crow does among the white, proclaiming their refugee status to everyone. In addition to this, the well-meaning, but un-thinking, donors of these garments, often fail to take the climate into account. A number of bales of used winter clothing were received in Saigon, where the temperature rarely falls below 80 degrees Fahrenheit, which could be used only to stuff mattresses and for cleaning rags. The money spent on their freight alone would have been suf-ficient to purchase many yards of the locally made cloth which the refugees themselves could have made up into garments, especially as many of them were tailors wanting employment.

Blankets are another item which is almost invariably sent although, in most tropical countries, these are not always the first essential, except for the sick and the elderly or if the disaster should have occurred high up in the mountains. The satin bound, pastel coloured variety are, in any case, of very little use in the mud and squalor of a refugee camp, and army-type blankets would be preferable.

The refugees' *immediate* needs, when the disaster occurs in a tropical country, are really very simple. Unless it is the height of the rainy season, housing is not usually the first essential but, rather, the means to cook their rice—which cannot be eaten raw—and the means to boil their drinking water to prevent epidemics such as cholera from breaking out. The type of three-legged cast iron cooking pot to be found in most markets throughout Afro/Asia, if issued to each family, would enable them to do this and would then free the helpers to cook for the elderly and the sick. In addition the refugees would, of course, require firewood, or in countries where this is very scarce simple oil stoves and kerosene, a leaf mat to sleep on and, in malarial areas, a mosquito net which should if possible be of the large type which encloses the whole family in a sort of room which helps to demarcate their area and ensures them a little privacy. With the addition of soap and disinfectant (best handled by the camp authorities) and, of course, food and possibly cloth to make into garments, these things are usually all that is required *urgently*. Nearly always most of these items could be obtained in the country concerned, and medical supplies might well prove to be the only things it was necessary to send in from outside.

How and where to purchase these goods and in what quantity is the type of decision the supplies officers of the international relief corps would have to make. It is the absence of such persons now which so often leads to the conflicting reports received by donor countries as to what exactly is required as well as to so much being sent out which is either unsuitable or unnecessary. "Necessity is the mother of invention", and refugees everywhere show great ingenuity in adapting things for their use, making lamps, for example, out of empty cigarette tins, with a piece of string inserted to act as a wick, and rain capes from the type of heavy plastic bag in which cement is supplied, since it is only necessary to

2 An improvised camp for refugees in South Viet-Nam, built on a sandbank, largely from tarpaulins.

slit them up one side. Plastic sheeting makes a useful tarpaulin and the various types of bamboo can be used for a thousand and one things from houses to furniture. The coconut palm is perhaps the most versatile of all: it provides not only food but edible oil, which can also be used to make soap, its fibre will make ropes and fishing nets, its leaves roof mats and its empty shells can be turned into charcoal. The more this type of initiative, based on local resources, is encouraged in the early stages of a disaster, the smaller will be the burden on the transport system, at a time when it will inevitably be hard pressed.

The first type of accommodation to be provided is likely to be very makeshift, even though the refugees themselves will help to make them as comfortable as possible. Nevertheless it is important that these temporary arrangements should not be allowed to become permanent.

The biggest problem in emergency relief work, however, is usually that of food. Throughout the world there are probably more prejudices concerning eating habits than over anything else. It is on record that, during the potato famine in Ireland in the last century, many people preferred to die than to eat the maize corn sent from America and, no doubt the same thing would happen here if after a disaster we were sent frogs' legs or snails to eat. Any drastic change in a people's diet needs long and careful preparation. It cannot be brought about overnight, especially when the recipients are in a state of shock and unable to take anything in. At such times it is important that at least something remains stable yet, all too often, governments seize the occasion of a disaster to unload their surplus foodstocks, regardless of whether or not these form part of the customary diet in that country. For example, in a recent B.B.C. programme on how to get rid of our surplus of potatoes, one speaker suggested that these should be processed and sent to India. Soya bean flour may be highly nutritious, but it is of little value if its distribution has not been preceded by an educational campaign to teach the women how to prepare and cook it, and dried milk needs very careful mixing if it is not

20

to form a lumpy unpalatable mess, because the exact proportions have to be very carefully followed. The larger tins, meant for institutional use, often contain no instructions on them at all, and even when these *are* printed many of the would-be users cannot read. In any case only certain types of dried milk are suitable for babies, who most need it, and, if the water with which it has to be mixed is contaminated, which is highly probable in refugee conditions, it can be extremely dangerous. Evaporated milk, in these circumstances, is far safer, if more costly, providing that it is supplied in small tins which will be used up before they have time to spoil. Where prejudices against drinking milk exist, as they do in a large part of Africa, they are not always without reason. It has recently been stated that Africans lack the enzyme known as lactane, which is necessary to digest milk properly, and, if this is true, it would explain their dislike of it. The American Public Health Association confirms this in a report of a survey carried out amongst Negro schoolchildren in America, 58 per cent of whom were found to suffer from cramps and diarrhoea after being given free milk at school.

More recently, the Protein Advisory Group of the United Nations System has issued a statement to the effect that it considers that this so-called "milk intolerance" has still to be proved. It advises that in areas where the population is not used to drinking milk, small amounts only should be served at first until the recipients become accustomed to drinking it, and until the problem of low lactase activity has been more thoroughly investigated.

Nutritional deficiencies are common in developing countries, and many people in Africa, where cereals usually form the bulk of the diet, will be deficient in protein and minerals and some vitamins, whilst in Asia, if people are given polished rice to eat, it will lead to the disease known as beri-beri. It is easier to counteract this, however, by issuing supplementary foods which can be added to the normal diet or vitamin tablets rather than by trying to carry out drastic changes in the diet itself, which would be a difficult task at any time and, in times of emergency, almost impossible.

Many countries have been carrying out research into

21

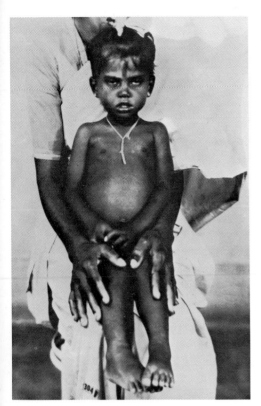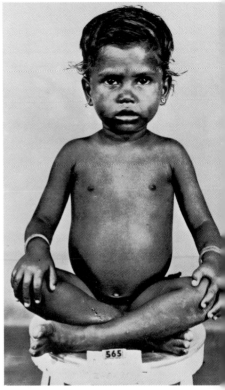

3 Nutritional deficiencies are common in developing countries. Millions of children in the Third World go blind each year from a lack of Vitamin A. (*a*) shows a $3\frac{1}{2}$-year-old Indian child suffering from malnutrition which has also affected her sight. (*b*) The same child 5 months later after a diet rich in green vegetables. (Royal Commonwealth Society for the Blind photos)

supplementary foods. New Zealand, for instance, has been experimenting with a type of milk biscuit and the National Nutrition Research Institute of South Africa has recently produced a food known as P.V.M.—from the proteins, vitamins and minerals which it contains. This food, which is meant to be added to the cereals on which so many African families live, consists of milk powder, eggs, soya beans and

22

deodorised fish and should prove most valuable in counter-acting protein and mineral deficiency. Similarly, if Vitamin B tablets can be issued to rice-eating people, when it is only possible to supply them with the polished rice we eat in the West, beri-beri will be prevented.

It has recently been estimated that, in the Southern and Eastern States of India alone, more than 14,000 children go blind annually from a shortage of Vitamin A in the vulner-able months immediately after weaning and that, throughout Africa and Asia and South America, the total runs into millions. The long-term remedy must be a change of diet (a cupful of green vegetables for each child every day is all that is necessary) but, in the meantime, 100,000 Units of Vitamin A concentrate given four times a year would counteract this disease, known as xerophthalmia, and the cost would be only 5 new pence a year for each child.

C

V Rehabilitation programmes for refugees

When the first emergency is over the temporary relief work will probably give way to a programme of a more lasting nature in which housing will be one of the first priorities, but exactly what type will depend upon the circumstances. If the disaster has been what the insurance companies like to describe as an "Act of God", the victims may only need shelter for a few days or weeks, until their homes have been rebuilt. If on the other hand it is a war situation, this may be necessary for several months or even years, as is the case in the Middle East now.

If the disaster occurred among the urban population it may have been possible to use the schools and other public buildings for temporary shelter. As things begin to return to normal, these will be required for their usual purpose and in rural areas where such buildings were probably not available, temporary camps may have been necessary from the start. A great deal, however, will depend upon the nature of the disaster and where it has taken place; in tropical areas, during the dry season, it is not an intolerable hardship to have to sleep out in the open if one has a mat to lie on but in the rainy season shelter will of course be essential. The rain will not be incessant, however, as people sometimes think, and even if several inches fall in an hour, there will be periods of sunshine. The worse feature will be the mud.

Whatever type of accommodation is planned, if it is likely to be permanent, it is desirable that the camp should avoid, as far as possible, the look of army barracks and be

4 Permanent houses being erected by the inhabitants of a refugee camp in South Viet-Nam. Although a great improvement on the makeshift accommodation shown in Figure 2, the layout resembles an army encampment and the sandy soil will make it almost impossible for the inhabitants to grow their own food.

built to look more like a local village with all the usual village amenities. If the traditional type of house is erected and local materials are used, the refugees themselves can help with the building programme, since most of them will have had experience building their own homes in the past, and this will give them an opportunity to earn some money for necessities.

The type of mud hut found throughout Asia and Africa, with local variations, such as being round in some parts and square in others, is one with which they will be familiar. It is very well suited to the climate and far cooler and less costly than the small concrete boxes with zinc roofs which we like to substitute and which require skilled labour to erect. These zinc roofs are exceedingly hot in the dry season, and in the rainy season the rain beats down upon them so noisily as to make conversation impossible in the room below unless it has been provided with a ceiling, and the cement floors which usually go with this type of building are cold to lie on in countries where the people prefer to sleep on the floor rather than in beds.

Many of the buildings that Governments erect, not only in the refugee camps but as part of rural development schemes, are far too grandiose for their purpose. Rural people everywhere are frightened of hospitals which are all glass and concrete and, in Africa, patients will often creep away to lie in the dark huts behind, provided for the relatives who always accompany a sick person to hospital, since these are so much nearer to their home conditions. The great mission doctor Albert Schweitzer realised this, which is why he always resisted the well-meant attempts on the part of his less experienced helpers and well-wishers, to modernise Lambaréné.

If it is felt that in building a refugee camp or village the opportunity ought to be taken to show the people how to improve their homes, this could be better done by bringing in piped water supplies, to save the drudgery of carrying it, and by providing proper sanitation, which would cut down the incidence of disease due to faulty hygiene—though it should be remembered that the squatting type of latrine is

5   A refugee village, as opposed to camp, in the Mekong Delta in South Viet-Nam. Here the conditions are much closer to those the villagers were accustomed to before the emergency arose. There is land for farming, and a fish-pond to provide much-needed protein.

preferred throughout Afro/Asia, and that it may be a long and uphill task to get the people to use any type of latrine at all.

Finally, paradoxical though it may sound, in carrying out this building programme, except perhaps in the provision of immediate temporary accommodation when speed may be essential, it is desirable that machines should *not* be used. The man-power situation in most of Afro/Asia is the reverse of ours. The need is not to find substitutes for high wages and scarcity of labour but, rather, to give employment to the many who may otherwise starve. This is true at any time, but is especially so during disaster situations. Since time is not usually of paramount importance once the immediate emergency is over, it does not really matter if one hundred men take two days to do what a machine could have done in one. What does matter is that employment is found for those men.

One of the greatest problems that most refugee programmes have to face, if the refugees are unlikely to be able to return to their homes in a few weeks' time, is their integration into the local community. At first their plight will have aroused much sympathy but, as time goes on and the presence of many thousands more people than usual in the area sends up prices, differences will inevitably arise between the refugees and the local inhabitants, especially in places where land is scarce and they themselves are also at near starvation level. This will be exacerbated if some of the refugees, who may be politically motivated, are using the camps as centres for guerilla activities, and, if these refugees are not nationals of the country in which they have taken refuge, these activities may prove exceedingly embarrassing to the Government who has befriended them.

In this type of situation it is advisable to try to keep the refugees as occupied as possible by organising educational programmes and the like. Literacy classes might be provided for the adults, for example, and formal schooling for the children, to keep them out of the mischief into which it is only too easy for them to fall in camp conditions. It is also a good idea to teach the young men and women a trade by means of vocational classes or they will gradually drift away from the camp, which will then be occupied only by the very young, the very old and the infirm, and this will bring many problems in its train. It may be possible to find persons who can act as instructors for these programmes from among the refugees themselves. Social workers will also be needed, both to keep the records of people in the camps—without this they might not qualify for public assistance—and to help them with the many personal problems they will undoubtedly have, ranging from the whereabouts of other members of their family to the loss of all their possessions. Medical workers will also be essential to help to prevent the spread of communicable disease by inoculation and vaccination programmes, and to see to the health of the people in general and especially that of the mothers and children.

Whenever conditions make this possible, it is also desirable that an agricultural programme is started to encourage the people to grow their own food, particularly as many of them will probably be farmers anyway. Unfortunately this is not always practicable, since in countries where farming land is already very scarce—which nowadays is nearly everywhere—the camp will almost certainly have been built on unproductive waste land or even sandbanks along the coast—as many in South Viet-Nam are—and it will be difficult to grown anything in these circumstances.

All of this has been written in the assumption that the emergency is one of manageable proportions. Much that has been said can only be a counsel of perfection when faced with the magnitude of the upheaval with which India had to cope when ten million refugees from East Pakistan were added to her already overstrained economy, and mostly in a State that was facing great political and financial difficulties before their advent. Many of the refugees were, of course, Bengalis themselves and this helped to create a bond of unity between them and the local people, but even so it was very much to the credit of the people of West Bengal that they showed so much sympathy and forbearance and were so willing to share their own already meagre stocks.

29

Villages which formerly housed only a hundred or so families found that their numbers had increased to three times as many almost overnight and not all of these refugees have gone back to Bangladesh.

Now that there appears to be a faint gleam of hope that peace may be achieved in Viet-Nam, if it is arrived at by means of some sort of coalition government in which the Communists will also be represented there will almost certainly be a mass exodus on the part of those people who left Hanoi for South Viet-Nam at the time when the country was partitioned. Having already fled from the Communists once, they are unlikely to remain if there is any likelihood that the Communists might take over in Saigon, and yet where are they to go? The fate of these people and of those in the Middle East—to name another danger spot— may ultimately decide the fate of the world as we know it today.

Are they to spend the rest of their lives in refugee camps or wandering round from country to country? Some have been doing so for twenty years. Are they to be absorbed into the population of the country in which they have taken refuge and, if so, who is going to help that country to bear the burden of it? Or are they to be dispersed to other countries under a controlled emigration scheme and, if so, which countries will be willing to accept them? They are usually the least skilled members of the community and the least able therefore to make a contribution to the country which takes them in.

The problem is a pressing one and the peace of the world may well depend upon a solution being found before it is too late.

VI Aid given by governments to developing countries

The second thoughts that many people are beginning to have about the suitability of much of our relief aid are repeated when it comes to considering our overseas aid in general. In fact it might not be too far fetched to claim that the often unsatisfactory nature of this has contributed, in part at any rate, to some of the political disasters which have occurred in recent years notably in what is now Bangladesh, where the aid given at the time of the earlier cyclone disaster was so badly mismanaged by both the Pakistan Government and the would-be helpers that the consequent break away from West Pakistan was almost inevitable, and much of the very large sum of money raised at that time has still not been disbursed.

Before going into the question of aid however we ought perhaps to list those countries usually classified as "developing". The United Nations Organisation gives 25 countries where the *per capita* income is below £38 a year and these are regarded as being in special need, but the term is generally taken to cover all countries in Africa (except Southern Africa), all in Asia (except Japan and mainland China, Korea and Turkey), the countries of the Caribbean and those in Central and South America and the islands in the Pacific. Eighty per cent of the world's population live in these developing countries, but it receives only ten per cent of the world's wealth. Every year the gap is widening despite all the efforts to close it, and the rich countries are getting richer and the poor countries poorer. Robert McNamara,

31

President of the World Bank has pointed out that, from 1960–7, the rich countries have *added* to their annual income a sum far greater than the *total* income of all the underdeveloped countries in Africa, Asia and South America.

Aid is a subject which inspires many conflicting views and the reasons for giving it are complex and not always well thought out, but Jean-Marie Domenach has expressed them very clearly in his book *Our Moral Involvement in Development*, published by UNESCO. Far too often, however, the approach to the whole subject is coldly analytical with the human aspects almost completely ignored, and a great deal of the aid given can be ascribed to the type of enlightened self-interest which is shown in John F. Kennedy's often quoted remark that "if we [the free Nations] cannot help the many who are poor we cannot save the few who are rich".

Governments also frequently give aid or withhold it as a political weapon, as for example when Britain withdrew the assistance offered to Tanzania because President Nyerere was striking out in a direction of which we did not approve (although Tanzania's progress since then and its concentration on developing its own resources has become a source of inspiration to many of the other African countries).

The decision of the United States Senate, in October 1971, to end all foreign aid emphasised this attitude. The Bill was defeated by an unusual combination of isolationists and liberals, the former stung by the unconcealed rejoicing on the part of some of the developing countries at America's defeat in the United Nations Assembly over the expulsion of Nationalist China, the latter because they have long wished to switch from bi-lateral to multi-lateral aid administered through international organisations such as the United Nations Organisation itself. In the debate Senator Frank Church was reported as saying that "[our aid] has been a spreading money tree under which the biggest American businesses find shelter when they invest abroad". Items in the defeated Bill were said to have included some 341 million dollars for Cambodian funds and arms for Israel, and 144 million dollars for the United Nations Organisation. Why should the people of the Third World be expected to be grateful for aid of this nature—even if perhaps the leaders of some of their more shaky regimes may have cause to be? It is not contributing to their well-being, but is mostly political in intention.

Much was made of press photographs at the time of the fighting in what is now Bangladesh which showed refugees existing inside large concrete drainpipes, but these conditions, shocking though they were, were probably not very far removed from those in which these persons were living before they became refugees. Anyone who has seen the slums of Calcutta, where the homeless eat, sleep and even die in the streets, might wonder whether humanity can sink lower, and it is surely with problems of this nature with which overseas aid should primarily be concerned. It should surely be an attempt to raise the standard of living of the many millions of people in the world today who live in dirt, disease and poverty through no fault of their own, but because they are victims of economic circumstances outside their control for which the West is not always free from blame. Poverty is the soil in which unrest grows and from which refugees result. As *The Times* said recently "the survival of the weakest is everyone's business".

A spokesman for one of our Banks, has said that, although millions of pounds have been poured into the developing countries in the way of aid, they seem to be worse off now than they were ten years ago. This is unfortunately true, and it is due as much to the wrong direction which our aid has taken as to faults on the part of the receiving countries—which is what the speaker implied. The West has far too often confused "aid" with "trade" and has placed far too great an emphasis on the necessity for industrialisation in countries which were predominantly agricultural and, although it is now increasingly recognised that this was a mistake, the damage has been done. It is disappointing that the United Nations Organisation, in spite of signs that it had come to recognise this and in spite of the talk of an entirely new approach to the Second Development Decade, has in fact served up very much the same mixture as before.

Whilst the man in the street in Britain and in other

countries is convinced that the developing countries exist
on our charity, and whilst more and more people are
inclined to say now that "charity begins at home", in reality
our overseas aid in Britain has not yet reached the figure of
1 per cent of our Gross National Product, which is far
below our recommended target. The report of the Commission on International Development, headed by Lester
Pearson, laid down ten major objectives for the next decade
and urged that official aid should amount to at least 0.7 per
cent of the Gross National Product by 1975—to many a
shamefully low figure when it is appreciated that the average
per capita income in the developing countries is only 200
dollars a year against an average income of 2,000 dollars in
Europe and 4,500 dollars in North America. Even allowing
for the fact that the cost of living is far higher in the West
than in most developing countries and that much that we
regard as essential is not necessarily so, this gap is far too
great for many people not to feel very unhappy about it,
especially as every year it is increasing and there are those
who say that it is now too late for the developing countries
ever to catch up.

Our efforts, too, to find overseas markets for our con-
sumer goods have made matters worse. We have encouraged
a desire for such things as colour television, cars and washing
machines which very few people in developing countries will
ever be able to afford and have thereby bred discontent.
"Civilisation" to the Eskimos of Barrow in Alaska now
means a cold store where they can buy frozen dinners—with
the outside temperature at minus 31 degrees—and water
melons at 8 dollars each.

Essentially, the purpose of aid should be neither to look
for an export market nor to buy political alignment, but to
help developing countries to help themselves. One method is
training programmes which take into account the needs of
the country, and the social and economic conditions pre-
vailing.

Another factor which should not be overlooked when
trying to assess exactly how much aid is given to developing
countries is the practice of charging high rates of interest on

34

6   The essential purpose of aid should be to encourage self-help. With the help of the International Labour Organisation, FAO and UNICEF, the Tunisian authorities have launched a rural pre-vocational training programme. Some 30 centres, including 3 for girls, receive almost 1,500 young people each year under the scheme. They are given general education and preparatory training for different kinds of rural occupation. Each centre adapts its training to local conditions. Here two Tunisian peasant girls learn how to prune fruit-trees. (ILO photo)

the loans that are made, so much so that it has been said that the service on these alone absorbs almost half the flow of total aid. It is small wonder therefore that when there is a change of government the new leader frequently repudiates the agreements entered into by his predecessor. In addition, much of this aid has strings attached to it in the form of stipulations that the money must be used to purchase the required equipment or machinery from the donor country.

Britain is not alone in this, and the same is true of most other donor countries. France, for instance, appears to give much more generously than we do, until it is realised that the published figures include administrative payments made to the overseas departments and territories which are still part of France, whilst in Viet-Nam the American economic presence can be said to have been almost as disastrous as the actual fighting. The arrival of many thousands of American civilians employed in the Agency for International Development's programme and earning as much in a week as most Vietnamese can do in a year, together with the presence of the armed forces, has inevitably forced the cost of living up to such heights that it is now impossible for a Vietnamese labourer to live on what he is paid, so that corruption and dishonesty are rife. Many millions of dollars are spent on aid, both in Viet-Nam and in the neighbouring countries, but a large part of this returns to the States in the form of the salaries and allowances paid to the American personnel administering that aid. The actual benefit to these countries themselves, in terms of hard cash, must be a surprisingly small one when these sums have been deducted, but this, of course, is also true of the other countries where specialists from overseas are employed, not only of America.

To anyone working in the field of development aid, it is a rather sick joke that it is far easier to ask for, and to obtain a grant of several hundred thousand pounds than a more modest sum like two hundred. It is also true that because of the slowness with which such aid is given, the two hundred pounds originally asked for will probably have to be doubled before the work is completed. One of the reasons for this is, of course, that it is administratively much easier for government officials to deal with one super scheme and between governments, than with many smaller ones at district or even village level. A giant hydro-electric project will not only provide many opportunities for profitable contracts but it may also help to maintain the balance of world power, which is always the concern of politicians. It should not be forgotten, however, that the financing of these schemes often strains international relations to breaking point. It was America's withdrawal from the Aswan Dam project which sparked off the Suez Canal crisis.

Theoretically, the provision of controlled irrigation, which a dam may make practicable, will be of as much benefit to the rural population as the cheap power it will provide will be to the often, as yet, non-existent industries. In practice, however, this is not always the case. Not only may the villager find himself very much worse off, through the loss of his land and his compulsory removal from the area, but he may even find that his livelihood has gone also, as has happened to the fishermen in Egypt, where the swiftness of the water flowing down river from the new dam is not only causing serious erosion of the banks (and of the Mediterranean coast), but has destroyed the fishing industry and therefore a source of cheap protein for the people. The fish, it is reported, now taste of mud. In addition the silt, on which the fellaheen has relied for centuries for his farming land, is no longer carried past the dam, as was the case with the earlier and lower one, so that a drastic re-appraisal of the whole agricultural position is now necessary, and there is growing concern among the medical profession at the way in which the snail which spreads the debilitating disease of bilharzia is becoming established in the side canals. To state all this is not to decry what is undoubtedly a great technical achievement, and one upon which Egypt itself was determined, but one may be permitted to wonder whether the fellaheen has not had to pay too great a price for it all.

When one thinks of similar occurrences in other countries such as the ill-fated ground nut scheme in East Africa, it is difficult to escape the conclusion that far too many of these plans are the product of desk-bound urban minds living far from the scene of operations. In Britain, for example, we send aid to more than one hundred countries, but only in the Caribbean and in the Middle East do we at present have Development Divisions on the spot, though it has been announced recently that more are to be set up. It is noteworthy that it is in these two areas that our aid programmes appear to be the most successful.

Some of the factors which reduce the effectiveness of overseas aid, too, are ones which are outside the control of the receiving countries themselves. The price increases which inflation has brought about in many Western countries has in effect meant that there has been a concealed cut in the aid received by developing countries since the money now purchases far less than it would have done formerly, and devaluation has also had this effect. The oil-producing countries have hit back by increasing the price of their oil, but most of the others, whose products are not so vital to the West, have found that there is very little that they can do about it. Malaysia now has to export more than twice as much rubber as she did in 1960 in order to be able to purchase the same amount of manufactured goods.

Finally and perhaps most urgent of all, there is the situation created by the so-called population explosion. By the end of this century, if the present birth rate continues unchecked it is estimated that there will be 8,000 million people in the world, of whom 6,000 million will be in the developing countries. Every day, in the world, 180,000 babies are born. Some developing countries are perhaps more aware of this problem than are some governments in the West. India and Pakistan, to name two of them, have had official birth control policies in operation since 1960, and thirty countries now subscribe to these, but religious scruples, poverty, and in some cases sheer ignorance and lack of concern for the future, prevent more people and countries from participating. Unless something can be done soon however to attempt to control this increase universally, even if overseas aid were trebled and the so-called "Green Revolution" were

38

to become twice as effective, these measures could still not counter the effect of all these extra mouths to feed.

A parallel situation exists in the present ruthless exploitation of our natural resources without regard to the needs of future generations. Environmental control is becoming as necessary to the survival of the world as birth control, or we may soon reach a position where the scarce materials may have to be rationed. The concern that people throughout the world are beginning to feel about this situation has been clearly brought out at the recent United Nations Conference on the Environment held in Stockholm at which Mrs Gandhi blamed the ecological crisis upon the policies of the affluent nations, which, she claimed, had assaulted nature in the name of progress and particularly for the profit motive. With 90 per cent of the world's metals being used by less than a third of the population, the advanced countries have already closed the door on development for the rest. As Nigel Hawkes pointed out in an article in the *Daily Telegraph* magazine it is estimated that existing *known* reserves of oil will be exhausted by the year 2001 at the present rate of consumption, that mercury will run out by 1984 and the reserves of zinc, lead and uranium by 1988. The U.S.S.R. is the only advanced nation which is self-sufficient in resources; the others will face a crisis (which could very well lead to the Third World War) if, one day, the developing countries tire of sending their raw materials overseas to raise someone else's standard of living.

D

VII Aid for overseas development

Much that has been said in the previous chapter also applies to the various overseas projects administered by the United Nations Agencies and the many non-governmental voluntary organisations now working in the field of rural development. Bearing in mind that the latter are in the hands of their donors, which must to a certain extent govern their line of approach, they usually handle a situation more quickly and more flexibly, and show a greater understanding of the human factors involved, than government departments. Unfortunately, however, in recent years, these organisations have also shown a tendency to concentrate on the bigger schemes to the exclusion of the smaller ones.

The United Nations Organisation also assists developing countries through its various specialised agencies, usually working through the government of the country concerned but increasingly through some of the non-governmental organisations as well.

The Food and Agriculture Organisation launched the Freedom from Hunger Campaign in 1960 to draw attention to the problems of hunger and malnutrition in developing countries. There are now Freedom from Hunger Campaign projects in many countries in the Third World. The United Nations Development Programme, which was established in 1966 to co-ordinate the several types of technical co-operation programmes carried on within the United Nations system, also offers assistance in the form of experts, training, and equipment, as well as surveys and studies intended to

40

7 A Freedom from Hunger Campaign project in Liberia. The
country has 700,000 acres of freshwater swamps fed by running
streams. When the swamps are cleared and systematically
irrigated, they can be made to grow improved strains of rice at
comparatively low cost. The system is particularly suited to
Liberia's predominantly wet climate. (FAO photo by G. Tortoli)

prepare the way for investment and technical training.

The United Nations Children's Fund was first established on a temporary basis for relief work in war-devastated countries, but its mandate has been extended for an indefinite period, almost all its aid is for long-range programmes, chiefly for mass health campaigns, maternal and child welfare, child nutrition and education, and the activities of the World Health Organisation, another United Nations specialised agency, are mostly devoted to helping to control disease and to improving general standards of health and nutrition in developing countries.

The Economic and Social Council (known usually as ECOSOC) which is responsible, *inter alia*, for co-ordinating the work of these specialised agencies has set up four regional Economic Commissions for Africa, Asia, Europe and Latin America to assist in the Social and Economic development of those areas.

The last of the major United Nations specialised agencies is the United Nations Educational, Scientific and Cultural Organisation (UNESCO). For some years now UNESCO has administered a Gift Coupon scheme which permits individuals and groups to choose a project to assist from a list drawn up by UNESCO. These people then collect funds to buy special coupons, known as UNUMS from UNESCO appointed agents in their own country and they are sent to the organisers of the project they have chosen, the UNUM being used by the recipients as a sort of international currency which enables them to buy the equipment or materials they require. No project is included in the programme unless it has been approved by the authorities of the country concerned, so that donors can be assured that the project they are supporting is worthwhile and that the money will be used properly and carefully.

This has been a most valuable scheme, which has already assisted more than 500 projects, but it has one defect in that it ignores a vital principle in community development, that of self-help. The emphasis is on people from outside sending the money into the country as a gift rather than on the people themselves raising the money or even part of it.

UNESCO also operates a second scheme which has proved of great value to scholars everywhere in overcoming the problem of foreign exchange. In this Book Coupon scheme, which is run on very similar lines to the Gift Coupon Scheme, UNESCO makes it possible for people wishing to purchase books, scientific equipment, or educational films from countries other than their own, to obtain the foreign currency for this by purchasing UNESCO coupons from specially appointed dealers in their own country. These coupons, which range in value from one dollar to one thousand, are then exchanged by the bookseller receiving them for their face value in his own currency. The total value of the coupons allotted to each country is of course restricted both by the willingness of the government of that country to participate in the scheme and by the size of UNESCO's hard currency reserves. Nevertheless the scheme has done a great deal to overcome the difficulties which would otherwise have been encountered by universities and scholars needing books from overseas. It should be stressed, however, that in this scheme, unlike the Gift Coupon Scheme, there is no element of charity. The person requiring the book must find the money to purchase it himself, and he is helped only by the provision of the necessary foreign exchange.

One of the great problems facing most Rural Development Officers in many Afro/Asian countries is how to obtain equipment needed for a project if it is not manufactured locally, since even if they have the money to purchase it from overseas they are not always permitted to send this out of the country. It is these circumstances which so often lead to requests to the West for grant aid or else for the equipment to be sent as a gift, but neither of these courses is desirable if the spirit of self-help is to be encouraged. An extension of the UNESCO Book Coupon Scheme to cover the purchase of simple agricultural machinery could also, in these circumstances be of the very greatest value. There is precedent for the provision of such things as water pumps, corn mills and padi-hulling machines and simple farm tools in that these

43

already qualify for inclusion in the Gift Coupon scheme, but if UNESCO felt that, in this context, they were outside its terms of reference possibly they would come within those of the Food and Agriculture Organisation.

Whilst foreign exchange is, of course, a problem even for the West at present, UNESCO already underwrites this in the outright grants it makes, which would not be so necessary if this scheme were to be adopted. Abuse could be prevented by limiting the value of the coupons which any one scheme could purchase and they could be issued under the same conditions as UNUMS are. Such a scheme, putting the emphasis on self-help but affording them the means to practise this, could do much to make developing countries more independent of outside aid.

When it comes to outright grant aid, at present this is almost always for one hundred per cent which fails entirely to take into account that people value far more highly what they have had to work hard to obtain than what they have been given, however contrary this may be. It is desirable, whenever possible, to involve the people themselves in any plans for their welfare, and they are much more likely to be so if a grant is on a pound for pound footing instead or, alternatively, if it is stipulated when the grant is offered that the community must also be prepared to contribute a part of the cost in the form of voluntary labour or materials, which can be assessed at their cash value and credited to the scheme. If a fifty-fifty division is felt to be too high, having regard to the circumstances of the people concerned, it is still advisable that some sort of contribution is made, even if it is as low as five per cent. Only in this way will the people feel a part of the scheme, for the element of charity which will otherwise be present is as damaging to their self-respect as soup kitchens and the like were to the poor in England in Victorian times.

Finally, revolving loan funds, instead of outright grants, are perhaps the best way of making a very little money go a very long way. In the Cameroons, as described in greater detail in Part Three, such a fund, established with a capital of only £200, eventually provided more than £6,000 worth of corn mills for the use of the members of the women's societies there. Ten of these mills were purchased initially at a cost of £20 each and the women given a year in which to repay this loan. As the money was repaid more mills were purchased so that in the end more than 300 societies had benefited from the original £200. Because it was their own property the mill was looked after far better than other equipment which had been given them by the Agricultural Department, and which was often left out in the fields to rust on the assumption that it would be replaced free when it was no longer serviceable.

These loans funds do not involve as much book keeping as might be thought, although the majority of the women were illiterate they kept a close tally on payments and, by doing so, were learning to handle money and to appreciate co-operative principles.

Whatever the type of aid given, however, whether it is in the form of an outright grant, a partial grant, a gift of equipment or a loan to purchase it, more attempt ought to be made to ensure that the recipients know from whom it has come, especially when it has come from private sources.

To say this is not to want to reap thanks or cheap publicity but because, in the interests of international friendship, the people should know that other people in Britain, or America or Scandinavia, care enough about them to want to try to help them. At present most gifts, when they reach their destination, are shrouded in anonymity.

There is a story told of an occasion when, after a disastrous flood, many bags of rice were given to an Asian country by America. Since it was a multi-national relief operation the rice was carried to its destination in Russian lorries. After a time the Americans realised that slogans had now appeared on the sacks, in Chinese characters, but it was some time later before they discovered that these said "this rice is brought to you by Russia". The tale no doubt is apocryphal but it does illustrate the point that Russia, at any rate, seldom fails to make its contributions known.

VIII Personnel for work overseas

The day of the Colonial Service is now over, never to return, but the gap which it has left cannot be said to have been entirely filled by the multiplicity of organisations which have taken its place. The current Directory of the Economic and Social Council of the United Nations Organisation lists 41 agencies as working in Africa alone (see also Appendix, p. 125) and it requires an expert to keep up with them all.

The best type of colonial officer lived with and for his people. His attitude may have been paternalistic—and that is outmoded now—but he spent a large part of his life in the country, studied its customs and spoke the language, and above all he provided continuity, which is what is most lacking nowadays. Nor were all colonial officers administrators; the majority were specialists working as medical or education officers or as builders and engineers.

Amongst the organisations who send youthful volunteers overseas, the British Volunteer Programme, which includes Voluntary Service Overseas: the Peace Corps and Service Civil International are three of the biggest and best known. Similar organisations have been formed in a number of other countries and the United Nations Association's International Service is also now sending volunteers out to work with the U.N. specialised agencies. All these organisations are based on excellent principles, do much good work and are now placing much greater emphasis on qualified volunteers than was always the case in the past, but even so the youth and comparative inexperience of many of the

46

volunteers sent out must mean that, very often, they gain more than they have to give. This is not too serious an objection, however, if their work broadens their outlook and enables them on their return to help to spread a better knowledge of the developing countries amongst those who have never been overseas. The changed circumstances, however, can bring problems. The young colonial officer not only went through a course of training before he went out but had also to serve a cadetship before he was left on his own, and he was always part of a team with all the resources of government behind him. Today the young volunteer is often working without supervision from the start and not only can this make things unnecessarily hard for him, it can also lead him into several pitfalls. In his enthusiasm and his desire to identify himself with the people with whom he is working he may, for example, "go native" and try to live like them, an exceedingly well-meant gesture which seldom succeeds and is seldom appreciated. A foreign woman dressed in a sari can rarely carry it off. She only serves to emphasise the grace with which the Indian women wear theirs and is often a source of ridicule to them. This is not to advocate that such a volunteer should remain isolated from the people he is trying to help but to suggest that there is a *via media* in this as in most things and that he would do better to accept that he is a Westerner and therefore lacks the resistance to dirt and disease which the local people will have built up over the years. If he fails to recognise this, he may well be invalided home before the end of his tour, a quite unnecessary martyr in these days of prophylactic medicine.

Another type of volunteer, found particularly among those engaged in field work, may cultivate an image of toughness, dressing in a dirty pair of shorts and very little else, washing infrequently and shaving only at the weekends. He does not realise how offensive this will be to most Afro/Asians who, when water is available, will bathe at least twice a day and who frown upon any unnecessary exposure of the body. No Afro/Asian soldier would dream of wearing the shapeless tropical overalls issued to the British and American troops overseas. He would immediately take them to the local tailor to have them altered to fit, and his wife is chosen as much for her prowess in starching and ironing them as for her other more obvious charms.

Even when a volunteer steers clear of these mistakes, and the majority of course do so, he is sometimes shocked by the poverty and distress he encounters probably for the first time in his life, and is too eager to change everything immediately and too inexperienced, as yet, to have much to put in its place. His greatest handicap, however although it is no fault of his, is the shortness of his stay since it is improbable than he can remain longer than a year, although he cannot be expected fully to gain the confidence of the people in that time. Even if he has conscientiously studied the country and its customs and language before he came out, the people themselves need time to study him, and until they are convinced that he really has something to offer them they will remain politely non co-operative, especially if he is seeking to make drastic changes. When this volunteer, at the end of his tour, is replaced by some one else the people have to adjust themselves to a different personality and quite possibly a different working method. Small wonder, therefore, if some schemes fail to get off the ground at all; and unless volunteers can stay for at least two years they are better employed on something finite which they can complete before they leave, such as a dispensary building or on a teaching project in a school. Community development projects are best left to more permanent workers.

Many of the organisations working with volunteers have now shown themselves aware of this problem. The enthusiastic but somewhat naive volunteers sent out in the early days have been replaced by graduates with far more to offer the people they are seeking to help and many are now staying for longer periods than formerly. Whatever the shortcomings there is no doubt that the immense good will and dedication that these volunteers bring to their work is in itself a most valuable contribution to international friendship and understanding.

An important point to be borne in mind by volunteers, and by specialists, is that the conservatism of the local

8   Tadla region, Morocco. One of the most effective ways of convincing farmers of the importance of using fertiliser is through demonstration plots. A farmer is given fertiliser and selected seed for planting a portion of his field, and the remainder is planted in the traditional way. When the crops mature, neighbouring farmers are brought to see the spectacular differences between the two plantings and the improvements achieved by selected seed and fertiliser. This is the basis of the Freedom from Hunger Campaign's industry-sponsored fertiliser programme, now under way in 26 countries. (FAO photo by F. Botts)

inhabitants may be a barrier to improving standards of living. The local people should not feel that they are being coerced into using new methods; and a practical demonstration of improvements which can be made in crop and livestock may be a tactful way of introducing them to changes.

49

In addition to these volunteers, who mostly work on a pocket-money basis there are the many trained field workers employed by the various international relief organisations, such as those who have combined to form the Voluntary Committee on Overseas Aid and Development in Britain, Church World Service, The Pontifical Council for Emergency Relief and Development, the League of Red Cross Societies and the bodies associated with the World Council of Churches.

The workers from these organisations are, of course, older and more experienced, and since they often live many years in a country they have time to get to know the people and do not have to rush them into making decisions which they have not had time to consider properly (which is often the reason why a development scheme fails). They usually speak the local language fluently and are sometimes authorities on the local customs. Their limitation, when there is one, is that they are tied to a particular line of approach by the aims of the organisation they are representing, which is often associated with the Christian Church, or else may be sponsored by their home government. Even if they themselves are anxious to help non-Christians this may not always be acceptable to countries whose national religion is not Christianity.

The third group of workers are the specialists attached to the various United Nations Agencies and those engaged by governments on a contractual basis (mostly professional men and technicians), the salary of the latter sometimes being paid by their home government, but more often by the government to whom they are accredited. Whilst these perhaps afford the nearest approximation, nowadays, to the former overseas civil servants, unlike them they rarely do more than one tour in a country, which may vary from one or two years to four or five, according to climatic conditions and the terms of their contract. Unless they are employed on something finite like the provision of a town water supply or the building of a hospital, they too will be leaving just as they have become valuable. They may subsequently be offered a second tour in another country, but the methods that have proved successful in, say, Africa, may not be equally so in Asia and vice versa. And knowing that they are unlikely to see the fruits of what they are planting can be disheartening to some and can encourage others to experiment more recklessly that they might do if they were going to have to live with their mistakes. Unlike the colonial officer of old, who *was* the Government, their loyalty lies with that of their own country whom they rely on to pull them out quickly should any serious difficulties arise.

The specialists working for the United Nations Agencies sometimes stay no longer than the volunteers already mentioned. As experts they can, of course, dispense with some of the preliminaries necessary in the case of less experienced people, but nevertheless there is no real short-cut to human relationships, which must be given time to develop, and the shortness of their stay is a weakness here too. There is also a danger that, moving about in so many countries, they are tempted on arrival to fit the facts to their theories and to try to repeat a programme which has been successful elsewhere, although the circumstances may have been very different. When time is a consideration, it is usually much quicker to start afresh from the ground up rather than to attempt to build on existing foundations. There is however a danger that the resultant building may not blend well with the landscape and this tends to be true of U.N. programmes overseas, where too much has sometimes been attempted in too short a time. The appointment of these specialists is occasionally resented by the local staff. While the United Nations Organisation pays their salaries and often donates the equipment they bring with them, the local government must provide their accommodation—usually to a fairly high standard—and their transport, and they also enjoy diplomatic privileges, all of which are the cause of some jealousy on the part of those who must accept much lower salaries and far fewer emoluments. Such experts can be of great help to developing countries, but their reception is sometimes rather mixed.

Aid and self-help

Some overseas countries are already carrying out their own development schemes. India has a fine tradition of "service for the people" (Sarva Seva Sangh) started by Mahatma Gandhi and continued by Vinoba Bhave, who has linked the many streams of thought together in the Sarvodaya movement. The movement's chief aim is the redistribution of land for the benefit of the landless. Land, when donated, is taken into common ownership and a village council set up to administer it, one twentieth being given to those who had no land before and the rest cultivated by individual landlords. From these "Gramdans" larger units known as "Blockdans" and "Districtdans" have now developed and it is possible that Bihar may soon become the first "Statedan". The movement has political undertones—it aims at the decentralisation of power—but it proves that the peasants can be persuaded to work together for their own good if the approach is correct.

Newspapers have recently reported that, in future, students in India may have to undertake a period of compulsory service in a type of rural reconstruction corps and, providing that they do their work willingly and do not despise the villager because he has not had their opportunities for education, this is an admirable idea.

Many developing countries now have excellent Agricultural Extension Services, notably the Philippines and Malaysia. In Sarawak, extension workers live together as a team in the Longhouses, remaining there for several months at a time, the girl member teaching domestic subjects and the man agriculture and animal husbandry. In Malawi the Ministry of Agriculture has launched a campaign to increase crop and poultry production.

Whilst overseas workers undoubtedly have a contribution to make to rural development in Afro/Asia, as in the case of relief work, the most valuable contribution can be made by persons who are natives of the country concerned. The question of their training is an important one, and the majority now study overseas. Cambridge and Reading

52

9 The Ministry of Agriculture in Malawi has launched a country-wide campaign to increase crop and poultry production. Through its agricultural extension service, an educational programme is being carried out by extension workers who are in touch with farmers in the rural areas of the country. Here an extension worker demonstrates the use of fertiliser to farmers. (FAO photo by F. Botts)

10 Education in home-making subjects for girls in India. Pupils should be taught to use the type of equipment and materials they will have access to in their home areas. (ILO photo)

universities run courses in rural social development and so does the Institute of Social Studies at the Hague, as well as a number of other universities. It is doubtful, though, whether this can be of very great benefit to the student since the conditions he is studying are so far removed from those he will encounter when he returns home. He too often becomes discouraged by the disparity or becomes so Westernised that he does not go back at all. One wonders, too, how courses of this nature can possibly cope with students from all over the world. A course in, say, mathematics is presumably the same whether the student comes from Africa or Asia, but when it comes to community development student backgrounds may differ so much, one would have thought, as to make a combined course impracticable. Girls studying Home Economics are taught to use electric cooking stoves when the districts to which they are returning may not have electricity at all, and men are taught highly mechanised farming techniques although the terrain in the country where they live may be totally unsuited to these. They return home bent on carrying out a social revolution which, even if it is practicable and desirable, cannot be brought about overnight and will almost certainly bring them into conflict with the village elders. The elders are not always the stupid reactionary old men their adversaries like to portray them as. They have very great influence in the community and, once they have been won over to an idea, their support will probably turn the scales in its favour. They have learned, however, that an over-ambitious or ill-thought-out project will put the clock back, not forward, and they are right to be cautious. Experiments must not only be successful they must be seen to be successful. It is a tragedy when the respect which exists for old age throughout Africa and Asia is undermined by students returning from overseas with a thin veneer of Western culture and very little else, and it would be far better if these students could be trained in their own or neighbouring countries where conditions are similar to their own. Once trained themselves, it is a simple matter for them to carry out the training of village leaders as long as care is taken not to require too high a standard of education for admission purposes. Many of these leaders are illiterate through no fault of their own but because schools did not exist in their neighbourhood when they were young, and this applies even more to the women. Illiteracy should not be equated with unintelligence. It is not essential for them to have to be able to work out the cubic capacity of a pump before they can be taught how to use it, since this the organiser can do if it is necessary, and all they need is a simple course lasting one or two days covering only the particular project in hand at the time. If later a new project is introduced, then they can attend a second course. Most illiterates have phenomenal memories and have no difficulty in retaining, almost verbatim, what they have been taught.

IX Social and religious customs in developing countries

The importance we attached in the past to social customs still lingers on in the developing countries and it is therefore desirable that workers overseas should know at least some of the more important ones in the areas to which they are going. This will help them to establish better personal relationships with the people there. Even in Europe we are more welcome if we know that in French theatres we should tip the usherette, that in Austria one gives trinkgeld to the lift attendant and that in Greece, in a restaurant, one should leave a small tip on the cloth for the assistant as well as on the plate for the waiter. In the same way, to know that in many African countries it is extremely discourteous to offer or accept a gift with the right hand is to start oneself off in the right direction.

The list could be continued indefinitely. One should not attempt to seat oneself higher than a Chief or cross ones legs in front of him. One should not pat an Eastern child on the head (this can be most offensive) or allow one's dog to run up to Muslims who, if it should lick them and they are strict in the practice of their religion, will have to go to the Mosque to be purified. Nor should one photograph Muslims without their permission, since it is against their religion. This is, in any case, a dangerous practice in many areas, for if the person photographed should happen to die shortly afterwards the death may be blamed on the photographer.

Schoolchildren in Africa who turn their back on you when addressing you, or mumble through their cupped hands, are not being impolite—on the contrary, they are showing you that they consider you a person of supreme importance. The Chinese, who offend us by blowing their nose noisily through their fingers, think our use of handkerchiefs disgusting. No Asian would dream of keeping his shoes on inside the house, still less the temple or mosque, but Europeans often cause offence by doing this. Nor in some countries is it desirable to praise a baby too much: the spirits might be envious and do it some harm, and it is much better to say how ugly and ill-favoured it is and then they will go away.

An Eastern bride must wear an expression of extreme sadness throughout her marriage ceremony, while on the other hand a bright smile should always accompany the bearing of bad news such as the breakage of your best piece of china. The Western press recently made much of a photograph of a robber, about to be executed in Nigeria, apparently laughing unrepentantly in the face of the priest who had come to give him the last rites. More probably he was, literally, "putting a brave face on it": a nervous rigor is often to be seen on the faces of Africans when distressed or frightened.

As well as remembering customs such as these, we should not forget that our approach is often too direct. It is extremely impolite in most of Africa and Asia to contradict someone. A person who enquires if he is on the right road to so and so, having, by the way he has phrased his question revealed that that is where he wishes to go, will almost invariably be told that he is, even if in fact he is going in the opposite direction. This is not due to stupidity but to a desire to please and it is much wiser to put such questions positively, for the correct answer would have been given if he had asked which was the road to so and so.

It is also discourteous to an Asian to refuse an invitation, so that, even if he is well aware that it will be physically impossible for him to be present on the day for which he has been invited, he will not say so when the invitation is proffered (especially if it is a verbal one). He will be politely vague at the time and fail to turn up on the day, unaware, of course, that, this is to us much ruder.

On the other hand both Africans and Asians will ask questions on subjects which we, in our turn, consider impolite. What our salary is, for example, how much we have paid for something, how old we are and so on.

But, above all, the thing that the West is perhaps most guilty of is our failure to realise the importance of that untranslatable term "face". It should never be forgotten that someone like a Chinese bank clerk, unwisely scolded in public for some small clerical error, can feel so deeply about it that he is capable of committing suicide.

The passage of time is something which means very little overseas. A request, which one assumes has been forgotten since it has met with no apparent response, will be dealt with two or three years later exactly if it had just been made and with no apology for the delay. Punctuality, however, is perhaps the thorniest problem of all. In many countries the correct arrival time is one or two hours after the time stated but in some others it is an hour earlier!

In countries where clocks and wrist watches are not universally available the people show remarkable skill in telling the time by the position of the sun but they will be badly thrown out when the sky is overcast.

Whilst only a good linguist will probably be able to master the language in the year or so which is all the time most volunteers going overseas have at their disposal, if they can at least give the customary greetings in the language of the country it will be much appreciated, and it is important to pay attention to the correct way to address people. In Malaysia, for example (and the same applies to most other Muslim countries, with slight variations) Che Rugayah binte Ibrahim is addressed as Che (Mrs) Rugayah. She is not Che Ibrahim, that is her father's name since "binte" means "daughter of". Her husband's name may be Yusuff but she will not use it, which makes it difficult sometimes to know who is married to whom. Similarly, in the case of Chinese women, Mrs Chua Eng Siong and Madam Teo Bee Kiaw can be one and the same person. In the first place she is using her husband's name, in the second she is using her maiden name but prefixing it with "Madam" to show that she is now married. In either case she would be addressed by the first name, that is to say as Mrs Chua or Madam Teo, for the next two names are used only by the family. On the other hand the reverse is true in Viet-Nam, Miss Tran thi Ngan is addressed as Miss Ngan, the "Tran" is a clan name.

Africans frequently have several names. If they are Christians they will have a Western one, such as Paul or David, to which they will answer at the Mission, but they will also have a tribal one and can adopt their mother's or their father's at will. Under no circumstances, however, should their personal names be called out aloud in public, if they are pagans, for fear of attracting evil spirits. When an official does this, for instance when he is checking the names on a register at election time, the person whose name is called will probably not respond even when he is standing there.

In the case of Indians, their names can give some idea of their religion. If their surname is a biblical one, such as Abraham or Isaac, they are probably Christians; if it ends in Singh they will be Sikhs (the female form of this is Kaur) whilst Chatterjee, Sen and Dutt are typical Bengali names, and someone with the surname of Patel will usually be from Gujarat. All these people will of course be Hindu.

When it comes to eating, customs throughout the world vary greatly. In most countries it is most discourteous not to eat anything which is proffered, however unsavoury it may appear, and a loud belch is obligatory in a number of countries to express one's appreciation of the meal. In Africa it is customary before drinking to pour a libation on the ground for the gods. Muslims should always be given the opportunity to wash before meals, and Muslims should never be offered pork to eat or Hindus beef. Both Hindus and Buddhists are often strict vegetarians and some will eat nothing but vegetables and rice, whilst Muslims do not smoke or drink alcohol.

However poor a peasant may be he will share his food with you and will be offended if offered money. It is wise therefore to carry with one, as far as is practicable, bags of salt, sugar, tea or coffee as these are all luxuries which will be most gratefully received. In the same way when gifts of food are brought to one's house a gift in kind should be given and not money.

These may seem small points to some people, and possibly they are, but it is extremely important to pay due attention to religious customs and ceremonies. We are inclined to insist on our own religious holidays, such as Christmas, but to be impatient when the local people wish to observe theirs—although it must be admitted that, in a multi-racial society such as Malaysia, where Muslim and Buddhist, Christian and Hindu work side by side, life seems to be one long holiday!

Hinduism is the oldest faith of all and Hindu society is the product of many ancient races and cultures. It is a caste system, although less importance is attached to this nowadays, and Hindus believe in an all-pervading, omnipresent God and also in a variety of other gods and goddesses whose images are to be seen in their temples. Life is a cycle of lives in which man's destiny is determined by his deeds, from which he may seek relief by ascetic practices, failure to achieve this release, however, means re-incarnation after death to a higher or lower form of life.

The fact that the cow is a sacred animal to Hindus and must, therefore, be permitted to wander where it likes is one of the biggest handicaps India has to face in its agricultural programme since there are many thousands of these unproductive animals eating up the scarce grazing and often mere bags of bones who must not under any circumstances be slaughtered.

The Sikh religion is an offshoot of Hinduism which came into being some 400 years ago and Jainism is another offshoot dating back to the 6th century. The Jains hold that all life is sacred, even that of plants, and refuse to kill the smallest insect. Care should be taken, therefore, not to offend Jains by swatting flies or mosquitos in their presence.

Buddhism was founded in the 6th century B.C. It accepts

61

the Hindu doctrine of a cycle of lives and teaches the way of salvation through ethics and discipline. A man's actions control his destiny after death, but the idea of a universal God pays no part in this religion. There are two main streams; the first and purest form, the Theravada (or Hinayana) School of Buddhism, is practised in Ceylon, Burma, Thailand and Cambodia, whilst the Mahayana school is prevalent in China and Japan, and Lamaism is practised in Tibet and the neighbouring countries, where the monks and priests wear dark red robes as opposed to the saffron coloured ones by which they are distinguished in the other countries.

The religion of the Muslims—Islam—was founded by the Prophet Mohammed in the 6th century and can be said to have started as a Christian heresy. Even now Christ is recognised as a prophet but not as the Son of God. A devout Muslim has a duty to pray five times a day at set times, turning in the direction of Mecca but not necessarily in a mosque. It is sufficient if he has washed and is standing in a clean place (hence the prayer rugs). He must also give alms generously to the poor, must keep the month-long fast of Ramadan and once in his lifetime he must try to visit Mecca. When he has done so can use the title of Haji which gives him great social and religious prestige.

Muslim women are often kept in purdah, that is to say they are confined to certain rooms in their house and do not go out except on rare occasions when they must be enveloped in a garment which leaves only their eyes exposed. However, the farther one travels from Mecca the less strictly this is observed. Thanks to the efforts of Mrs Liaquat Ali Khan, wife of the first Prime Minister of Pakistan, purdah is no longer practised there and was abolished in Turkey by Kemal Ataturk, and the Muslim women in Malaysia and Indonesia generally lead much freer lives than those in the Middle East.

A form of animistic worship is to be found in some parts of Africa and Asia. The people believe that the world is populated by good or bad spirits and that natural objects such as plants or trees may be their abode. The influence of good spirits has therefore to be invoked to drive away the evil ones, whilst messages from the spirit world can be conveyed by dreams or omens or by the state of the liver of a pig or fowl after it has been slaughtered. If the omens are inauspicious a journey will be postponed until they are favourable. Before growing things are cut down, at harvest time for example, the spirits must first be placated with gifts.

Other religions to be found out East are Taoism and Confucianism. Taoism preaches the worship of a "Supreme Being" conceiving each human being as a grain of sand in an immense desert. Life is but a short stay on earth, and wealth and glory are ephemeral things. Since Taoism seeks the suppression of earthly desires and ambitions, adherents are possibly the least likely to welcome change of any sort. Confucianism is an ideological and ethical system based on the concepts of moral order and the development of the moral qualities of a man towards himself as well as towards other human beings. From an early age Confucians conform to strict rules of behaviour which include filial devotion, conjugal fidelity, friendship, fairness, justice and charity. Ancestors are venerated and therefore followers who are driven away from their villages by war, as in South Viet-Nam, will always try to return to the family graves when conditions make it possible.

In all these religions festivals still play an important part. In countries with a predominantly Chinese population the lunar New Year is the great occasion and lasts for several days. Houses must be swept from top to bottom and all debts paid before the New Year enters, an event which is greeted by deafening blasts from fire crackers hung from balconies. Since babies are counted as one year old at the time of their birth and, since everyone has a birthday at the time of New Year, a child born only two or three months before New Year's day will be counted as two years old after it.

In Muslim countries the great occasions are the feasts of Id al Kabir and Id al Fitr. The latter occurs at the end of the month-long fast of Ramadan, during which Muslims must not eat or drink even water between the hours of sunrise and sunset. In countries where the temperature may be as high as 100 degrees Fahrenheit this can be a very real hardship, and Muslim staff in offices etc., needed to be treated with special consideration during this time.

Diwali is a Hindu festival, occurring in October/ November, which is celebrated by the ceremonial lighting of lamps and by illuminating the fronts of the houses, whilst gifts are also exchanged. During the spring festival, in March/April, which is known as Holi, bonfires are lighted and red powder scattered over the celebrants, whilst decorated chariots are dragged through the streets by devotees. It is from the immense chariot used in the procession at Jagannath that our term "Juggernaut" arises. All the major temples will also celebrate their own festivals during the year with processions in which the temple elephants will take part.

The Buddhist New Year, in Theravada countries, takes place also in March/April and in Thailand coloured water is squirted over the participants. The main festival, however, is that celebrating the birth, death and enlightenment of Buddha, which takes place in April/May and at which captive birds are released in memory of his compassionate nature.

All these festivals are fixed by a lunar calendar and therefore vary as much as our Easter but, for all practical purposes, these countries use the same Western calendar as we do.

X Some suggested projects for rural areas

There are many simple projects which villagers could carry out for themselves, often with little or no supervision and at small cost, which would, nevertheless, make an enormous difference to their well-being. The West could help them greatly in this if, when giving aid to the governments of their countries, they could stipulate that some of it, at any rate, must be used for development projects at village level. An additional factor to recommend such a course is that aid given to a small community, where everybody knows everybody else, is far less likely to be misappropriated than it is in larger schemes where no one knows who is responsible for what.

Some ideas for projects are given in this chapter. It will probably be necessary, in most cases, to carry out a pilot scheme first for which a trained organiser may be required, unless it is possible to send someone from the village on a short preliminary training course. It is difficult for uneducated people to grasp abstract ideas, and villagers who are told that a pump, for example, could lighten their labours considerably are not likely to believe it until they have seen such a pump in action. They may also need help in obtaining it, and are unlikely to be able to instal it without assistance. Finally they will almost certainly be unwilling to pay for it. Once it has been shown to meet their needs, however, it will be progressively easier for the organiser to "sell" the idea to the surrounding villages and they will be much readier to pay. If, when several villages have installed these pumps, the organiser holds some demonstrations to show them how to service them, his presence should no longer be necessary and he should be free to repeat the proceedings in another area. In this way the maximum use is made of his services whilst the only expenditure, apart from his salary, will have been on the pump used for the pilot project.

Most of the projects suggested here could be handled in this way, whilst several may not need paid organisers at all. Many of them can also be carried out with local materials. We sometimes tend to think in terms of imports when working overseas, forgetting that in the past in England we adapted ourselves to local circumstances, building in stone in the Cotswolds but in wattle and daub or brick elsewhere according to local resources. This state of affairs still exists in developing countries and almost every district will have its own methods, and the invaluable bamboo in one or other of its many varieties will be available almost everywhere. In Sarawak a scheme to run water into a Land Dayak village by gravity feed from a nearby stream was held up for many weeks for lack of the special joints needed to join the lengths of imported polythene piping together. Eventually one of the villagers, on his own initiative, manufactured them out of bamboo and it then became obvious that hollow bamboo could also have been used for the piping. The fact that it would not, of course, have lasted as long as the polythene piping was of little importance when there was no shortage of free labour or bamboo, and the scheme would have cost virtually nothing. The villagers had not thought of such a project for themselves solely because they did not understand the idea of gravity feed and, not being able to take a level, did not know at what point in the stream the pipe should be inserted. Once shown this they could have carried on unaided—as a number of villages did later on.

There are many similar instances where local materials are as serviceable as imported ones. Crushed ant hills, for example, beaten down, make quite as good a floor as cement.

If one were to make a list of priorities for rural projects in

11   The provision of water is a very high priority in rural
projects. (*a*) shows all the water which was available for both
drinking and washing for a village of about 200 people in West
Africa. (*b*) A simple inexpensive scheme appropriate for small,
remote villages. The spring that fed the pool shown in (*a*) was
led into this storage tank, which filled up during the night and
so provided drinking water for the villagers during the day.

Afro/Asia, most people would agree that the provision of water should be the first. Sometimes there is too much of it and steps have to be taken to control flooding, but more often there is too little. In Africa it is quite common for women to have to walk several miles to find water in the dry season and it is then often drawn from a brackish pool in which their clothes are also washed, and there is much ill-health as a result. Even when a hydro-electric scheme is planned for the area, if the village is a small and remote one, it is unlikely to benefit since the cost of running the piping in would be prohibitive. Officialdom is more likely to think in terms of moving the village, and it will therefore have to look to its own resources. If it is hilly country a simple aqueduct can often be constructed by digging a trench to run gradually down the side of a hill, leading the water from a stream into the aqueduct or else a pipe can be inserted into the stream, as was done in Sarawak. If the flow is only small, it may be necessary to build a storage tank as well so that the water can collect there overnight. If possible such a tank should have a filter, but even if this is not practicable, the water in it will be much cleaner than water which has been carried in receptacles which are used for innumerable other purposes, not always of a very hygienic nature.

If it is flat country, where these methods will not, of course, be possible, rainwater can be stored in artificial ponds, known as "hafirs" in some countries, which the villagers can dig for themselves, first lining the hole with polythene sheeting and then laying on top of this small sausage-shaped bags filled with a mixture of cement and earth which, when the weight of the water has consolidated them, become impermeable.

In other cases a simple suction pump may be all that is needed to force the water up from a lower level. In a country like Borneo, where the longhouses are built high up on the banks of the rivers to avoid the floods, such a pump, lifting water directly into the longhouse, would prevent the accidents which sometimes happen now when a child or an elderly women slips on the muddy bank when going down to fetch water and is drowned.

68

Where there is a small water-fall a hydraulic ram can be used to lift the water and this has the advantage of requiring no petrol, which is difficult to get in remote areas, as well as expensive.

Wells are another possibility, and where the type of soil permits this, they can be of the time-honoured pattern where a bucket is lowered on a winch, or they can be covered and fitted with a small suction pump operated by the user. The latter method is the more desirable as it prevents the well from being polluted by dirty buckets or by children dropping things down it.

Bore holes and artesian wells are other ways of getting water, but they are both more costly and more complicated and will need technicans to carry them out.

Housing is probably the thing which would come next in most people's lists. In most cases the local materials should be quite adequate for this. Bamboo frames plastered with mud or mud bricks dried in the sun make convenient and cool houses. In a district where a laterite soil is available a "landcrete" or similar machine can be used to make bricks of compressed earth, mixed with cement if desired. These are more resistant to rain but the local houses are usually built with overhanging roofs to prevent too much rain striking the walls and damaging them. In these brickmaking machines the soil is rammed down into a mould by a lever operated by two men and several hundred bricks can be made in a day.

Generally, however, villagers will require little advice when it comes to building their homes. They will have been doing it for generations and, in that time, will have evolved a style very suitable to their climate; but help might be given in suggesting minor improvements. For example, most interiors are far too dark, the windows, which are of course without glass, having deliberately been made very small to keep out thieves, and screens of expanded metal wire would overcome this problem.

Then in much of Afro/Asia the cooking is done inside the houses on open wood fires. The smoke gets in the people's eyes and inflames them badly and, at night, when the people sleep round the fire, old people and children often suffer burns from rolling over into it whilst they are asleep. A smokeless cooking stove such as the Hurl stove designed in India, which can be made out of mud or cement, would do away with this whilst, in South-east Asia, if the "dapor" on which the women cook were raised up on legs there would be fewer cases of children scalding themselves.

The roofs of rural houses are usually of grass or of mats made from palm leaves and they are cool in summer and warm in winter. They are far more pleasing to look at than zinc roofs and much less costly. It must be admitted, however, that they are a bad fire risk, which a zinc roof is not and that the latter also affords a means of collecting rain water, which can be run off into storage tanks or into old 44 gallon oil drums placed under the eaves. This water will not be drinkable but will be invaluable for washing purposes, and if the drums are covered with small gauge wire mesh there is no risk of mosquitos breeding in them, which is the constant fear of Medical Officers of Health.

As much of the daily life in a village in the tropics is spent out of doors, it is difficult to attempt an educational programme in these conditions. There will be far too many distractions and it would in any case be impossible in the rainy season. If, therefore, the village is to have a school for the children, or literacy classes for the adults are contemplated, some sort of meeting hall is going to be necessary. It does not need to be an elaborate building. It can be of the simplest design, merely four posts supporting a roof of matting or grass with more mats forming the walls up to waist height, to keep out straying animals. If something more substantial is possible, however, it is most important that the villagers should be encouraged to build it. Far too often any money available for this purpose is used to employ a contractor who puts up a splendid building which, although it may become the showpiece of the Administration, will almost certainly be too grand for the people to use it freely.

Sanitation also should be given high priority on the list, although the villagers themselves will probably not think so.

Without any knowledge of elementary hygiene, they do not always realise how many of the diseases from which they suffer, and from which their children often die, are preventable. Such a programme would, of course, include the provision of latrines, but of which type will depend on the customs of the country. Except where the soil is too water-logged to make digging possible the pit type is the most usual and probably the best. The Western-style water closet, even if it is of the squatting type, is not usually practicable through shortage of water and because it can soon become blocked.

If piped water can be run into a village, then, when doing so, it is an easy matter to provide some stand pipes at head height which make simple showers. Cement troughs can also be made in which the women can wash their clothes instead of having to stand in the sometimes fast flowing river. Where they like to pound their clothes on a stone to get them clean, cement slabs can be provided beneath the stand pipes.

Roads are also something which might be tackled as a village project. Again, it depends upon the local circumstances and is more probably necessary in Africa than in Asia. It is quite astonishing how much can be accomplished when a whole village turns out to dig. Skilled labour is only required for the bridges and culverts and a route should be chosen which necessitates as few of these as possible. In the Cameroons, in one area, several thousand men and women were able to dig a road more than three miles in length in one day, although, of course it took longer to put in the bridges. These service roads afford a means whereby lorries can get into the villages to take out surplus food for sale in the markets, and also make it possible for the villages to be visited by the mobile health units which more and more are becoming a feature of rural life.

A problem in the case of villages built along a main road is the dust raised by passing vehicles which can become a serious health hazard. Eye diseases and respiratory troubles are very common in the dry season. To tar the whole length of these motor roads would be an extremely expensive

71

12 A fish farm in Godawari, Nepal. Carp and other local species are being bred in stream-fed ponds, to stock up local fish ponds. The Godawari Fish Farm is also an experimental centre, assisted by FAO, and aided by the United States, Switzerland, Israel and India. (FAO photo by C. Day)

proposition, but if the portion which passes through a village could be treated it would make a great deal of difference to the well-being of people living in countries where there is little rainfall.

In countries where shortage of water is not a problem, fish ponds are an excellent means of supplementing the diet of the people. The villagers, however, will need advice as to the best site for the pond and help in obtaining the fish fry with which to stock it. This is something with which the Agricultural Department ought to be able to help. Sandy or rocky soil should be avoided as it will not hold water well and, as the pond is dug, the earth should be piled up to form bunds round it. It should also be shallower at one end than the other, with a draining pipe at the deep end, screened to prevent fish escaping through it. Once the pond is filled with water, it should be allowed to stagnate and organic manure should be added, and when the water has turned green it is ready for stocking. There are several species of fish that can be reared in fresh water, of which carp and tilapia are the most common. The fish can be harvested easily when required and will form a source of usually much needed protein.

Finally, in many developing countries the people still practise crafts which could be put on a commercial basis and so afford them a living. Unfortunately this is not always quite as easy as it sounds. For one thing they are up against the mass-produced machine-made article in world markets, whose price will be much more competitive; and for another they are unused to commercial disciplines. Given an order for, say six mats in black and white measuring perhaps 3 feet by 4 feet, they will produce instead six mats in red and blue measuring 5 feet by 3 feet and when asked why will merely say that "they liked doing those better"! Given a contract for sago biscuits by a trader in the town, they will decide to put in fewer eggs one week—possibly because the hens are not laying so well—so that the quality declines and the trader refuses to accept the biscuits or to place an order again. Often beautiful work is done on very poor materials because this is all they can afford, and exquisite embroidery is done on coarse calico and beadwork on old shoe leather. These are problems, however, which a trained handicrafts organiser with a knowledge of commercial techniques ought to be able to overcome and, if a means to encourage the sale of local craftwork can be found, so that the rural people could have as much chance of earning their livings as people living in the towns, this might help to stop the drift from the villages. Some governments have, in fact, already set up organisations to encourage rural industries, notably Malaysia

73

and the Philippines, and it is to be hoped that more will do so.

The tourist trade ought to provide a market for these goods but it is sad to have to report that, so far, the tourist influence has only led to the production of cheap and nasty "Westernised" souvenirs at the expense of genuine craftmanship.

XI Mechanisation

In saying earlier that too much stress is laid on mechanisation in rural development schemes, this was not meant to advocate that we should rule out the use of machines altogether. Simple, uncomplicated machinery, preferably not dependent on electricity or petrol for its operation and within his ability to purchase and maintain can be of the very greatest assistance to a villager. It is when the machinery becomes so complex that it requires much money to purchase it and engineering skill to operate and service it that it is doubtful whether it is really desirable for remote rural areas.

In developing countries, where farms are often only three or four acres in extent and may also be widely scattered, the reaction of most agriculturalists from such places as America and Britain is immediately to suggest that these farms should all be grouped together in order to facilitate mechanised farming methods. This is very much easier said than done. What is overlooked is that not only will this alter the whole way of life of the people, but it will probably also lead to long and protracted land suits and much unrest.

We did not ourselves, in the West, jump from tallow dips to electricity in one generation. Why then should we expect people in the developing countries to do so now, and to go straight from sickles to combine harvesters? We still manufacture in Britain some of the machines that served us so well before the advent of the petrol engine and these simple, manually operated machines could still be of very great help in developing countries. In addition Japanese manufacturers turn out literally hundreds of small, hand-operated machines for almost every purpose from grain fans to peanut diggers as well as those suitable for small-scale industries such as coir processing from coconuts, and ropes, mats and sacks from rice straw. There are also processing machines for bamboo. These are all designed for use by the small peasant farmer or in cottage industries and could be of far greater help to Afro/Asia than the highly sophisticated and expensive equipment we use on our own farms. The peasant farmers of Japan and China, who use these simple machines, achieve some of the highest yields per acre in the world. Their farms are small by Western standards but intensively cultivated by the whole family.

The type of cast iron, hand-operated, grinding mill which is still found on some farms in Britain, first manufactured here in the middle of the last century, can still be of very

13   Land Dayak women in a village in Sarawak using a padi-separator. On the left is a Japanese hand-operated padi-hulling machine, and in the foreground an aqueduct made from hollowed-out tree trunks supported on a bamboo framework.

great use in those countries where, at present, the maize corn is either ground between two stones or pounded in a mortar to produce the flour from which porridge, the staple diet, is made. This is a task which takes a woman an hour or more a day, after returning from the fields, so that, having ground enough flour for her family she often does not bother about herself but goes hungry. The grinding mill can grind in twenty minutes sufficient flour for all of them for a week.

Similarly, in rice-eating countries, hulling the padi by pounding it is an equally laborious task. The result is that many women now carry their padi to the nearest rice mills instead to have it hulled for them. Not only do they have to pay quite highly for this but the millowner keeps the husks which formerly the women used to give to their poultry. The most serious feature of this, however, is that these engine-driven mills polish the rice to such an extent that the Vitamin B content is destroyed, and this leads to severe nutritional deficiencies in countries where rice is often all that the poor have to eat. Japan manufactures a hand-operated padi-hulling machine which, whilst more effective than the pestle and mortar method, does not remove too much of the outer husk, as the engine driven mills do, and this could be as useful in Asia as the corn mill can be in Africa. There are a number of similar machines which could also be of help, such as pedal-operated drum threshers for rice, and maize- and ground-nut shellers, all hand operated and none beyond the women's means to own as a group. An additional reason for using these small, easily operated machines in preference to large, commercially owned ones, is that they afford an opportunity of introducing co-operative principles to the people, since they are within the means of the village to purchase for itself.

In many countries where cultivation is done only by means of a hoe the people might benefit greatly from the introduction of the plough—not the multi-disc type drawn by a tractor which they could neither afford nor operate but the "ard" which has been used for centuries in North Africa and the East and which can be drawn by any draught animals

77

14 An improved seed drill in action in India. It is made from materials readily available to the villagers. (U.N. photo)

available or by the farmer himself. Tropical rain fed zones and arid and semi-arid areas do not require the vigorous tillage necessary in the more temperate zones. The natives of these parts know this, of course, and, over the centuries have evolved implements which are superbly fitted for their purpose even if they are not always as technically advanced as ours in the West and are cruder in their appearance. These implements are usually made by the local blacksmiths, and instead of endeavouring to substitute our own tools because we ourselves are more familiar with them, might we not instead help these blacksmiths to modernise their methods so that these traditional tools can be given a sharper cutting edge and a better balance, where necessary? When agricultural machinery *is* introduced, it is likely to be these same blacksmiths who will have to repair it so that any attempts to improve their technique now will not be wasted. Had the Rural Industries Bureau not carried out a similar programme in Britain, when mechanisation was first introduced, the village blacksmith would have disappeared from our villages by now.

There are of course many other inexpensive machines which could help rural people a great deal. In countries dependent on rivers for communication, and in others where there are only tracks for roads, the inhabitants would be greatly helped if outboard engines and bicycles could be sold at subsidised prices so that they could afford to purchase them. These outboard engines are easily fitted to canoes and mean that journeys upriver against the current, which formerly might have taken three or four days, can be completed in a matter of hours, whilst bicycles are a far swifter form of travel than walking and can be used to carry heavy loads. In parts of Nigeria they are licenced as taxis, the passenger sitting behind the cyclist, and of course out East the three-wheeled variety have superseded rickshaws.

In many parts of Africa and Asia, people still carry enormous loads on their heads, or backs, which could be put in light hand carts, or pulled in wooden sleds, if they were shown how to make these. If the tracks are too narrow for two wheels the Chinese wheelbarrow would overcome this. This has one large wheel in the centre which is balanced by a load on either side. Because of its construction, it is far more manoeuvreable than our Western type and can be used for long distances. In a number of countries, too, animals such as donkeys could be used as draft animals if the people could be shown how to train and harness them.

Water pumps could be invaluable for many projects and especially for irrigation schemes. The hand-operated type should be introduced wherever possible, since petrol is not easily come by in the more remote areas away from roads. Basically these are of three main types. Suction pumps will raise the water for some twenty feet or so, force pumps will be required if the distance is greater, and diaphragm pumps are usually used where the water is muddy or contains solids. In Viet-Nam the farmers there have adapted the outboard engine used on their sampans to lift water from one irrigation channel to another and small windmills can also do this.

Whatever type of machine is contemplated, one particular point needs to be emphasised. It is essential that the machines require very little skill to maintain, since this is usually the weak spot as far as most rural workers are concerned. Unaccustomed to mechanical things they will not service the machine regularly and when it breaks down as a result, they will use brute force to put it right, thereby making matters much worse. They may then find a local blacksmith or garage mechanic who will effect a most ingenious repair from improbable materials like an old cocoa tin and some four inch nails, but they will take much convincing that, had they only inserted some oil at the proper time, the break-down might never have occurred.

If it is felt that it is necessary to introduce more sophisti-cated methods of agriculture it is, of course, essential that proper training is given first and that instructors take into account their pupils' lack of familiarity with machinery.

When it comes to life in the home, this might be made very much easier for the women by the provision of good oil lamps. At present most Afro/Asian markets stock only the

15   A rural development programme in southern Chad assisted
by the International Labour Organisation. Through a network
of training centres in three provinces, two French ILO experts
train rural craftsmen needed for the repair and maintenance of
agricultural machinery. After training, the craftsmen return to
work in their own villages.
   The growing use of draught oxen in agriculture in southern
Chad means plenty of work for rural craftsmen. Here a former
trainee and his assistant repair an ox-cart. (ILO photo)

bush lamp, which is meant for use out of doors and gives a poor light indoors, or mantle or pressure lamps, which give a far better illumination but can cost more than most villagers can afford and can be rather tricky to light. The former requires a mantle, which is very easily broken, and the latter, a pressure lamp, needs methylated spirit to light it satisfactorily, and this is not always obtainable. The type of table, or hanging, lamp with double wicks and a glass chimney, which we ourselves used in our sitting rooms before the advent of electricity, and which are still manufactured, would be far more satisfactory.

In the same way oil cooking stoves could be invaluable in the many countries where wood is scarce and where the women now use dried animal dung for fuel which would be better saved to put on their farms. Here again the plain cast-iron type, with one or two flat wicks about three inches broad are preferable to the pressure type, which are sometimes dangerous in inexperienced hands. The type of stove which has a tall metal chimney and circular wicks, and gives off a blue flame when lit, requires somewhat too delicate an adjustment for villagers unused to such things. The drip feed pattern of stoves are also inadvisable as they are dangerous if the glass container gets broken and smell badly if not kept scrupulously clean.

In some countries, in areas near the larger towns, butane gas cookers are now becoming available but they are beyond the means of the poorer people and they, too, have their dangers. Villagers are often not aware of the lethal nature of the gas and there have been cases of persons accidentally blowing themselves up and of others being gassed in their sleep through a tap being left on.

In isolated communities a very cheap transistorised radio set could be a blessing, on the lines of the so-called "saucepan" set which was in use in Africa in the fifties but now seems to be out of production. Most villagers find the ordinary sets beyond their means and too complicated to use since they require fairly accurate tuning. What is needed is a very simple set running off torch batteries and permanently tuned in to one station, where conditions make this practicable, or else provided with push button tuning to simplify this.

Some countries, such as Nigeria, issue sets to the headmen of villages. They are housed in a concrete pillar in the main street and switched on at stated times so that everyone can listen to them. In Sarawak, many of the Women's Institutes have their own sets to listen to the broadcasts which are put out specially for them.

Finally, mention should be made of the Intermediate Technology Development Group Ltd which was founded a few years ago in Britain with the object of assisting developing countries with information on low-cost labour-saving equipment and techniques for small-scale application. The Group issues a number of useful publications and two in particular should be of great help to volunteers going overseas to work on rural development schemes, they are *A Bibliography of Low-cost Water Technologies* and *Tools for Progress*, a guide to equipment and materials for small-scale development.

XII Literacy campaigns

In countries where large numbers of the adult population are unable to read and write, a rural development programme will be far more effective if it is accompanied by a literacy campaign.

The form that this may take will depend upon local circumstances, and the scale and degree of illiteracy present. If the campaign is to cover the whole country it will almost certainly need the backing of the government, but it should be possible to mount smaller campaigns in the villages with the help of the local school teachers. It is clearly of little use to attempt to raise the standard of living in other ways if the people are unable to understand fully what is being attempted. Audio visual aids have made things somewhat easier for illiterates these days but the radio is no real substitute for reading and, in any case, few villagers can afford one.

In most countries, when a census is taken, an attempt is made to find out how many of the population are illiterate, but the published figures are rarely conclusive. In the first place they are dependant on the criteria adopted by the enumerators, which can vary greatly. An adult who cannot read or write at all presents no difficulty, but what about the boy who after several years of reluctant schooling still cannot write his name? Is he classed as literate because he has been to school? And the adult who can read a few words but certainly not a newspaper? And are those who claim to be literate given a test to prove if this is true? For all these

16 A literacy class in Sarawak run specially for policemen's wives. From many different races and living in the barracks, with the minimum of housework to do and no land to cultivate, these women were bored and lonely until the classes brought them together and widened their horizons. (Sarawak Federation of Women's Institutes photo)

reasons the census figures are often somewhat suspect and can give only an approximate idea of the size of the problem in each country. Generally speaking, however, unless a person is able to read at least a thousand words he cannot truly be regarded as literate. He will need a vocabulary of this size to be able to read most newspapers to keep in touch with current affairs and it was probably for this purpose that he came to the classes in the first place.

In considering literacy programmes it is also necessary to make a clear distinction between those designed for adult students and those which are really only a substitute for a school programme, which will be attended mostly by children. These latter programmes will certainly be better than nothing, but they can only be regarded as a poor alternative to formal schooling because, although the children may learn to read and write through them, they will learn very little else. Without guidance they will be too young to know how to supplement their knowledge with judicious reading, if indeed a library is available to them, which is improbable.

In cases where the literacy campaign is intended for adults, it is usually inadvisable to admit children, at any rate under the age of, say, fourteen. Their parents will often ask for

17   A literacy programme for adults in the Cameroons. In Douala, the Young Christian Workers have founded a Labour College. Mothers of school-children at the Douala primary school Renaissance Nationale learn to read and write in the evening under the guidance of teachers trained at the Labour College. (ILO photo)

them to be allowed to attend because literacy classes are usually free, and, in many countries, schools charge a fee, and also because the children's hours of study will be shorter, leaving them more time to work on the farm. But it is not in the children's best interests if there are places in the local school, for the reasons given above, and their presence may be resented by the adults. Very few village elders, learning with difficulty, like to make mistakes in front of children who may often be young enough to be their grandchildren.

A difficulty which many literacy programmes encounter is that of the choice of language. Obviously a student will learn most quickly in the vernacular and it will be very much harder to teach him in a foreign language, such as English, but is it going to be possible to use the vernacular if it is not yet written down? For reasons of prestige many countries attempt this but they are not always very successful. Experts must first work on the grammar, devise an orthography and then write the text books. All of this is an expensive business and a lengthy one. Finally the student, after he becomes literate, finds that there are no other books in the language for him to read and soon lapses into illiteracy.

This does not apply everywhere, of course. In some countries there will be a lingua franca which will be understood by everyone even if there are other languages in use. In Nigeria, for example, Hausa is understood all over the North, and Swahili covers most of East Africa but what about a country such as West Cameroon where more than seventy languages are spoken, only one of which is written (Bali) and that not acceptable to the other tribes? None of these languages are spoken by more than seventy to eighty thousand people, often by far fewer, so that a literacy campaign in the vernacular would be wholly impractical. It is clear, that a campaign would have to be in one of the two official languages, English or French. This will naturally make things very much harder at first and will require teachers of a higher standard than might be necessary otherwise, but it will eventually mean that the successful student, when he is literate, will have the whole range of

Aid and self-help

English or French literature to draw upon and will also find his knowledge of the language useful outside his own tribal area.

The choice of language will influence the choice of text books, but whichever books are chosen, it is advisable always to use those written specially for adults. It is a great mistake to use books written for schoolchildren, since the text will be too childish in content and the method too leisurely. Few adults will be able to spare more than three or four hours a week for classes and cannot therefore afford the time to go over a point again and again as a child must do. Nor is it necessary for them to do so. Much that a child has to be taught an adult knows already from experience. He knows from his trading, for example, that two and two make four and has no need of diagrams or counting sticks to illustrate this; what he wants to be shown is how to write it down and how to read the numerals.

If he is taking the trouble to come to the classes he is probably doing so for a definite purpose, and this is where functional literacy comes in. His text books should be written so that, at the same time that he is learning to read, he is learning things which will be useful to him in his daily life and in his work. Just as, in foreign language teaching nowadays, the student is taught almost at the first lesson how to make a reservation in a hotel and how to order a meal in a restaurant, so his text books should employ technical terms which he may need to know in his employ-ment and should show him how to fill in the official forms which bewilder him so much and how to record his pur-chases. He does not need to have his interest held by stories, as a child does, at least not ones based on fantasy.

Whether or not these books are illustrated again depends a great deal on the country concerned. There is more of a tradition of graphic art in Asia than Africa, but if drawings are employed it is important that they are not too sophisti-cated, at any rate in the primer. People living in remote areas, who may never have seen a camera, do not always recognise even themselves in photographs, especially if they are in black and white. To them a tree is green and they do not

88

18   The need for practical education should not be overlooked.
Members of the Rural Improvement Clubs of the Philippines
plant fruit trees which are rich in Vitamin C in their gardens,
and they also cultivate vegetables. Members who have no
gardens use empty plastic bags or dried milk tins, which are
filled with mould made from coconut water and pineapple
peelings, and the vegetables are planted in them. The vegetables
grown are used mainly for the children's meals at the centres run
by the Rural Improvement Clubs. (The Rural Improvement
Clubs of the Philippines photo)

immediately identify it when it is illustrated in another
colour in a book. Similarly they will be confused by drawings
of things which have been "blown up" to three or four times
their natural size—a mosquito, for example—and will not
associate it with the mosquitos which are buzzing round
them. Nor is it advisable to use books which have been
written originally for another country. Students who themselves live in round huts are puzzled by drawings of persons
with different coloured skins living in square ones.

As they become more literate these strictures apply less,

but much quicker results will always be obtained if the text books are appropriate to the circumstances.

There is always a great need, too, for follow-up books, that is to say, graduated readers at the 1500, 2000 and 3000 word levels. There are plenty for schoolchildren but not so many for adults who prefer do-it-yourself books such as *Housing Building for Africans* or *How to Look after Your Money* to fiction.

The need for practical education should also not be over-looked, and this is already recognised in a number of countries. After the disastrous floods in the Philippines, school playing fields and even side-walks were used to grow vegetables, which nevertheless remained dangerously scarce. The members of the Rural Improvement Clubs were there-fore shown how to plant seedlings in such things as old olive oil tins, dried milk tins, and even in plastic bags, which were first filled with a mould made from coconut water and pineapple peelings. A good crop of vegetables, including green peppers and cauliflowers, resulted, and this was used to feed the children attending the day centres.

The method to be adopted by a campaign is another matter which will vary with the circumstances. Dr Frank Laubach's "Each one, teach one" campaigns have achieved specta-cular results in some areas, but this approach necessitates the use of the vernacular, and it is unlikely that it could succeed when the medium of instruction is a foreign lang-uage. The system employed is that a student, who has himself been made literate in a pilot class, then undertakes to teach another person to read and write who then teaches another person until everyone in the neighbourhood has become literate.

This is an excellent example of self-help, but when it comes to the employment of a language other than the vernacular, there is a danger of this becoming so garbled in transit as to be unintelligible at the end. Moreover whilst results are usually good at first, surveys have shown that whirlwind campaigns of this nature do not always ground the student well enough for him to be able to carry on by himself, with the result that many sink back into illiteracy again in later years. If it is possible to gain the help of local school teachers, a more formal campaign will achieve more lasting results. Some classes employ older schoolchildren as teachers but this is not entirely desirable, unless there is absolutely no other alternative, since, in the developing countries, the educated minority already tend to flaunt their superiority in the face of the less fortunate villagers. To ask men who may have positions of authority in the community to sit at the feet of schoolboys, metaphorically speaking, is unwise unless the schoolboys are prepared to show exceptional tact.

When it comes to the costs of the campaign, as far as possible the students should be asked to pay for their books, even if the sum asked is only a token one and below the actual cost price, otherwise they will not value them. It is desirable that the teachers receive some sort of honorarium, not sufficient to remove the principle of voluntary service to the community but enough to ensure that they are not out of pocket by taking the classes. Such a payment also affords a slight means of control to ensure that their attendance is both regular and punctual. If they are school teachers it may be necessary to impress upon them that they should not handle adults in the same way that they handle their schoolchildren. It is not unknown for them to do so, expecting the adult to put his hand up to answer questions and to stand up when spoken to, and it is this sort of treatment which is often responsible for the failure of a campaign.

Anyone, however, who has taken part in a literacy campaign will find it a most rewarding experience. The effect that the ability to read and write can have on adult morale is startling and touching.

XIII The part women can play in rural development

Since the majority of our Colonial Administrators were men, a practice that seems to be continuing in the case of most overseas appointments nowadays, there is a consistent tendency to underestimate the role that women can play in rural development.

The Western idea of the down-trodden female treated like a beast of burden and certainly not permitted to think for herself is mostly very far from the reality. Western women, in fact, have far less opportunity to rise to the top than their counterparts in Afro/Asia. It is likely to be a long time before we have a woman Prime Minister in Britain or any other Western country but both the governments of India and Ceylon now have women at their head and so has Israel. In South Viet-Nam women hold many important posts in commerce and industry and the women traders of West Africa exert considerable influence on the economy there. The Hong Kong diocese has been the first in the Anglican church to ordain women as priests.

In developing countries the roles the two sexes play are usually well defined. Man's traditional role in Africa was to guard his family against slave raiders and wild animals and it is largely because this is no longer necessary that he now has so much more leisure time than his women folk. It is still his duty, however, to provide whatever cash is necessary to purchase things which the family cannot provide from its own resources and, to this end, he is often away from home for many weeks at a time on trading trips or walking his cattle down to the coast to sell them there. In the majority of developing countries, except Muslim ones where purdah is still practised, subsistence farming is regarded as women's work, but the so-called "cash" crops—coffee, bananas, oil palms, cocoa, etc.—are the responsibility of the man, although he will expect his wife to assist him with the duller jobs like weeding. There are always clearly demarcated divisions of labour and these are not always the same as in the Western world. For example, in some parts of Africa the men will wash the clothes for the family whilst the women go to their farms and, in areas where there are no roads, a man will act as a carrier, for a cash payment, but will expect his wife to carry his load for him.

As *de facto* controllers of the land and providers of food for the family, the women have considerable authority, both in the home and in the community. In some tribes the Queen Mothers appoint the new Chief on the death of the old one, and in matrimonial disputes, if the woman refuses to work on her farm, the man will soon be brought to heel!

Despite all this, agricultural programmes are aimed almost exclusively at the men. Agricultural colleges accept only men students and the schools teach rural science to the boys but not to the girls. By adopting this policy and by attempting to get the men to take the women's place on the land, Western-trained Agricultural Officers too often fail to realise that they are destroying the whole established social pattern and worsening, not improving (as they often think), the lot of the women. The success of their programme will in fact depend on how well they are able to "sell" it to the women, since they are the farmers and unless they can be convinced of its value it is unlikely to succeed. This is not because women are slow to adopt new ideas but because they are realistic enough to know that they cannot afford to experiment on a four acre farm unless they can be reasonably certain of success; a harvest which fails is a disaster when there is nothing in reserve with which to feed the family.

In one country much time and money was spent on a programme to introduce coffee as a smallholder's crop. The coffee unaccountably failed to prosper until it was realised

93

19 Domestic science instruction in Sierra Leone. The training
of women in domestic skills is being promoted by the
governments of many developing countries, assisted by the
International Labour Organisation under its vocational training
programme. (ILO photo)

that, although the courses of instruction were being given to
the men, it was the women who were actually doing the
planting and that, not having been shown the correct way to
do it, they were digging holes which were too small for the
coffee plants, so that the tap root was being damaged.
Once they were allowed to go to the courses the coffee
flourished.

However, in urban areas, male and female roles have tended
to become Westernised, and women are given training in
domestic skills. The international organisations who offer

94

assistance are, on the one hand, providing a well-meant and useful training, but, on the other, reinforcing changes in the traditional way of life.

Increasingly nowadays the women in both Africa and Asia are forming themselves into societies run on the lines of the many women's organisations which, since the turn of the century, have done so much to transform rural life in the West. The popular belief that the Women's Institutes in Britain exist on tea and jam making is totally false. In the past fifty years they have done more than any other organisation to revolutionise life in the countryside, and if the drift from the land now seems to have been checked it is largely because, through the Women's Institutes, the rural woman's life is no longer one of lonely drudgery.

Any attempt, in developing countries, to carry out an agricultural or development programme will therefore be much more likely to succeed if the aid of such women's organisations, where they exist, is enlisted. In one West African country the Agricultural Department's policy was to prosecute anyone found farming down the side of a hill instead of along the contours. After several women had received prison sentences for this the mere sight of an Agricultural Officer was sufficient to make all the women take to their heels and remain hidden until he had departed. In these circumstances the agricultural programme hardly prospered, but once the Department had been persuaded to send agricultural assistants to the meetings of the women's societies there, to explain about soil erosion, contour farming was adopted everywhere.

The same stories can be told of other countries. Most rural women work far too hard to be interested in a society established solely for social or even educational purposes, but one which can offer them practical means of reducing their labours will always be supported.

In Sarawak, the women's institutes there are to be found even in the most remote villages in the Ulu, where women who have never had a chance to go to school have now learnt to read and write and, in addition to carrying out

Aid and self-help

improved agricultural practices, have been to the forefront
in helping with relief work at a time of natural disaster.
Everywhere rural women's organisations carry out social
welfare programmes (which in the West are left to the State),
sometimes raising money to help with school fees or running
their own kindergartens, and in other cases providing simple
hostels for rural women having to visit the towns. In India
they were in the thick of the work for the refugees from
East Pakistan.

The future of the developing countries may well lie with
the women, who are far harder working and more realistic
in their approach than most of the men. Dr J. E. K. Aggrey,
the famous African educationalist and first Vice-Principal of
Achimota College, used to say "educate a woman and you
educate the nation". This is equally true in the context of
rural development, for if the women's confidence can be
gained the whole family will participate.

XIV The Cameroons in the fifties

Whenever it is suggested that self-help should be encouraged in developing countries, it is often said that the people are not yet ready for it, and that they need pushing all the time to get anything done. To answer this type of objection, the final chapters of this book describe a project in the Cameroons where self-help was successfully encouraged. It is hoped that this may show that such projects are perfectly feasible with the right approach and the minimum of outside interference.

In 1952, when the programme which is described in the following pages began, the Southern Cameroons, as it was then called, was United Nations Trusteeship Territory, administered by Britain as part of Nigeria. In 1958 however, the country was given self-government and in 1961, with independence became part of the Federal Republic of Cameroun and is now known as West Cameroon.

The Bamenda area, where these happenings took place is some 300 miles by road from the coast and is one of the most beautiful parts of West Africa. It is high plateau country of an average height of four to five thousand feet and consists of rolling grasslands broken up by steep valleys and a number of mountain ranges of which the highest, Mount Oku, reaches to nearly 9,000 feet and is topped only by Mount Cameroon at the coast—the third highest mountain in Africa.

The road up from the coast, via Mamfe, is tarred for only part of the way. After Mamfe it rises steeply through jungle so dense that, in the rainy season, the sun cannot penetrate it to dry the road out and it soon becomes impassable: at all times it is too narrow and twisting to allow for two-way traffic so that vehicles must travel up one day and down the next. In the dry season, with luck, the journey could be completed in two days, in the rains it could take twelve hours to cover as many miles, the road deteriorating into a series of ever-deepening craters as each lorry in turn dug itself out from the morass. Even four wheel drive vehicles needed the help of powerful tractors to pull them through the mud and most had to be written off after two or three journeys in such conditions.

For six months of the year, therefore, Bamenda was virtually cut off from the coast. The alternative route now open was not then readily available since it necessitated crossing the border into what was then known as the French Cameroons, that is to say, the part of the Trusteeship Territory administered by France.

Up to the mid-fifties the road stopped at Bamenda Station, the Administrative Headquarters for the Province and all journeys past that point had to be made on foot or on horseback. Mail was head loaded by runners who took two days to cover the 65 miles from the Station to Kumbo Town in Nsaw. Even when the ring road round the Province was completed it was still usually necessary to finish a journey on foot even if it was possible to go part of the way by car. Many villages were three and four days walking away from a motor road and others were down inaccessible valleys or up on the hillsides.

The population of the whole country was then just under a million, almost equally divided between the coastal regions and the grasslands but, whilst the inhabitants of the former area were of semi-Bantu origin, those in Bamenda were negroid. The broken nature of the terrain meant that in the past there had been little communication between tribes resulting in a bewildering variety of languages. Out of more than a hundred vernaculars only one was written and, since this was that of the tribe the Germans used to help them conquer the territory before the First World War, to speak

98

or write it was not the best introduction to the other tribes who had not forgotten the role the Balis played at that time. As a consequence English was of necessity widely spoken and its pidgin form almost universally understood by the men, though most women spoke only the vernacular.

The Province is a well watered one, the rainfall varying from 65 inches to as much as 124 according to the altitude, whilst the maximum temperature in the lowlands is over 90 degrees falling to around 84 degrees in the grasslands.

The population was, and still is, an essentially rural one. There are no large towns, although several places including Kumbo are dignified by that title. Elsewhere they would usually be classified as large villages. Bamenda and Nkambe Stations were merely administrative headquarters occupied by a handful of government officials and missionaries. Kumbo and Wum, the largest "towns" in the Province, both of which had schools and hospitals, each had a population of about four thousand. In 1952 the life of the people, both men and women, was a hard one, especially that of the women. They worked in the fields during the hours of daylight (which, so near the equator, extended from roughly six o'clock in the morning to six at night) and then, when they returned home, had to prepare the evening meal for their families, often stopping on their way back to gather up large heavy bundles of fire wood or to carry water. Born to the mountains, they made shorter work of them than outsiders unaccustomed to the height, and thought nothing of walking twenty miles a day when necessary. In the absence of motor roads, distance was judged not by miles but by the length of time taken to walk it, just as the time of day was fixed, with remarkable accuracy, by the position of the sun in the sky.

Because of the height the people were not so malaria ridden as those at the coast, but the cold nights and the heavy rain in the wet season took their toll, and pneumonia, tuberculosis and other respiratory diseases were not uncommon. In the early 1950s most women wore little more than strategically placed strings of beads, but the men wore long black gowns covered with machine embroidery (done

99

by men—not women) and embroidered caps which pro-
claimed, by their design, which tribe they came from, as did
the cicatrices often cut on the women's faces. With increased
prosperity the women came to adopt the rappa rappa, a
length of brightly coloured Manchester cotton twisted round
their body in the manner of a sarong but, like a great deal
which is done in the name of progress, it was not an un-
mixed blessing. Unless it was washed frequently, which was
often not the case, it led to skin diseases like scabies, and
feverish chills also became much more common in the rainy
season from women sitting in their wet garments.

Subsistence farming in Bamenda, as in most African
countries, was in the hands of the women who maintained
small and sometimes scattered farms of three to four acres
each on which they grew the food for their families, whilst
their husbands provided any money which might be required for such items as salt by cultivating the so-called
"cash crops" such as coffee, or by making the long journey
on foot to Northern Nigeria to sell the Kola nuts which grew
freely in the Province. Sometimes, too, they went down to the
coast on trading journeys, whilst the Fulani drove their
cattle down there to sell them for meat and sometimes the
younger men went down to work on the rubber, banana and
oil palm plantations for a year or two to earn enough money
to buy a wife.

In terms of Africa the land in Bamenda Province was
fertile, if rather patchily so, but large parts of the grasslands
had been given over to cattle ranching. The women's farms
were mostly on the sides of the hills where they hoped that
they would be safe from the depredations of the cows, but
which had led to serious erosion. These cows belonged to
another race, the Fulani, a pastoral people who were brought
in from Northern Nigeria in earlier years, by the Administration, to provide a source of revenue by means of a poll tax
on their cattle. They were a beautiful and graceful people of
Hamitic origin with lighter skins and more aquiline features
than the other inhabitants of the area. Muslims of the Sunni
sect they rarely remained long in one place and were frequently involved in cattle disputes with the local people.

The scenery in Bamenda is very similar to the Highlands in Uganda, without the lakes. Immediately after the rains everywhere is a lush, fresh green, and the air is so clear that it is possible to see for fifty or sixty miles in every direction. As the dry season develops, the plains turn to amber and burnt sienna, and the sky clouds over from the smoke of the grass fires lit by hunters hoping to drive out the little game which is left in the country. Whole areas are devastated by this practice and a sudden shift of wind sometimes results in a village being burned down or an unwary traveller being burnt to death. The Harmattan wind from the Sahara desert blows at this time too, making people nervous and irritable and chapping their skin badly. Clouds of dust cover everything, and it is the least attractive time of the year even if travel is easiest.

The food of the people in Bamenda was reasonably plentiful but lacking in protein. Basically it was a better diet than that eaten down at the coast, but they lacked the fish which was naturally more easily available down there and the palm oil. To offset this however, they grew a variety of fresh vegetables such as cabbages, carrots and potatoes, but meat, although available, was eaten only on special occasions because of the cost. Rather scrawny chickens abounded but were tough eating and their eggs were saved to sell in the market, but were usually kept so long that a purchaser would find that at least half were bad. The principal item of diet was maize corn ground down to a flour to make a porridge called *foo foo* which was served with various relishes and vegetables.

Markets were held in all the main centres, that at Kumbo being famous even in Nigeria so that people came to it from far and wide. They were usually held every eight days and everything stopped on these occasions. Equating this eight-day week to the seven day calendar used in government offices and schools caused endless complications. Newspapers and radios were almost unheard of before transistor sets were introduced and news was exchanged on market day, with varying degrees of accuracy, whilst word of any special events travelled round the countryside with astonish-

20 The bamboo framework of a hut in Bamenda in West Cameroon. The walls will be plastered with mud and the roof thatched with long grass. These houses are a fire risk, but are cool inside and will last for a number of years before the thatch needs replacing or the bamboos rot.

ing speed by means of the talking drums or by shouting it from one hill top to the next, the Chiefs themselves employing special runners who often covered fifty miles in a day. Away from the main roads, on bush paths, a letter would sometimes be seen stuck in a cleft stick signifying that the bearer had carried it as far as he was going and that it was up to the next person passing that way to take it on. Such was the awe with which the written word was then held that these letters seldom failed to reach their destination—which is more than can be said for the mail service when it was developed later.

Houses were simple, grouped together in family compounds and dotted all over the landscape. There were very few villages in the English sense, and people lived as near as possible to their farms. The oldest houses consisted of a framework of bamboo over which mud was plastered, and grass was used to thatch the roof. The houses of such people as clerks and school teachers were usually built of sun-dried bricks with doors and window frames of timber, whilst the wealthier men's houses were usually of dressed stone with zinc roofs, the Chiefs' compounds often resembling small villages since each wife had her own hut.

These Chiefs, or Fons as they were known in Bamenda, were perhaps more influential in the fifties than they are now when many of their powers have been taken over by the politicians. The most important was the Fon of Nsaw. The best known, however, were probably the Fon of Bikom, as the result of the Commission set up by the United Nations to investigate the allegation that he had more than a hundred wives and the Fon of Bafut, who figured so delightfully in Gerald Durrell's *The Bafut Beagles*.

It was because of the importance of the Fon of Nsaw and because his tribe, numbering some 70,000, was the largest in Bamenda that it was decided to start the community development project described in the succeeding chapters in his area.

XV Life in Bamenda

Whilst anyone visiting Bamenda in 1952 would have agreed that it was clearly desirable that something should be done to raise the standard of living there, it was also apparent that this was not something which an outsider could expect to tackle immediately. It was first necessary to gain the confidence of the people and to look at their way of life in order to see how they could best be helped. In this respect the fact that the area had already been closely studied by Dr P. M. Kaberry, Reader in Anthropology at University College London, was of great assistance. Her book *Women of the Grassfields*, published a year or two earlier, was an invaluable source of information on local customs and saved a great deal of research and, therefore, time.

As a first step it was important to be on good terms with the Fon of Nsaw as no development scheme could hope to prosper without his support. His word was law within his own tribe. It was also necessary to look around and see who amongst the local people were likely to be good material for training as field workers since a great deal of the success of the scheme would depend upon these people and a careful choice was essential.

The Fon was an old man who had acceded to the throne as a youth in the days when the Germans still administered the territory as their Colony of Kamerun. He lived in the centre of Kumbo in a large compound of more than a hundred separate huts for his wives and the court officials, with a central building for his own use with a courtyard in which was a raised dais on which he sat to judge cases brought before him and where he received visitors. In 1952 these buildings were constructed of bamboo with carved wooden pillars supporting the grass roofs but they were becoming undeniably shabby and were far less resplendent than those of lesser Fons in the neighbourhood. This was a source of chagrin to the Nsaw people, but the Fon was deaf to their pleas that they should be allowed to build him something which they considered more in keeping with his status. One Christmas morning, however, the whole inflammable complex caught fire and was burnt down in a matter of minutes and the people's response was magnificent. Most villages keep stocks of sun dried bricks and these and other building materials were now instantly placed at the Fon's disposal and carried in by relays of men and women and, by nightfall on the same day, he was rehoused in a new three-roomed zinc roofed brick building. During the succeeding months, a new palace was erected, the Fon's permanent quarters being built this time of stone. The exact contribution to be made by each village in terms of cash and materials was carefully worked out, as was the labour quota, and the whole was a most impressive demonstration of the people's organising ability and of the importance that they still attached to the Chiefdom.

Under the Fon were the various court officials and the village and district heads who wore curiously shaped caps to denote their rank. It was necessary to be on good terms with them too, as it was with the Yas. These women, mostly elderly, had considerable influence in the community, maintaining their separate households and receiving many privileges otherwise accorded only to men, including that of wearing men's caps. They were known as "Queen Mothers" although, in fact, they were more often sisters and daughters of the reigning Fon or of previous ones. The Fon's wives, who numbered over seventy and who wore a circlet of cowrie shells on their head, were of far less importance. They were amongst the hardest working members of the community and responsible for farming the Fon's considerable estates. Many were wives in name only and would have been better

105

described as old age pensioners. They were wives of earlier Fons or of brothers of the present Fon, and had he not taken them in, as by custom he was bound to do, they would have starved.

Education was largely in the hands of the three Missions operating in the country, the Roman Catholic Mission, the American Baptists and the Basel Mission from Switzerland, all of whom ran schools in the Province whilst the first two also administered hospitals. Although there were now schools in even the most remote areas there was a high degree of illiteracy amongst the older men who had reached adulthood before this programme had developed, and amongst the women, since very few parents, even in 1952, were willing to pay to educate a girl child. (This created a problem for the younger educated men such as the school teachers who were reluctant to marry a woman who could not keep up with them but who could find few women who could even read and write.)

Although the intention of the proposed development scheme was primarily to help the women it soon became apparent that to achieve this it would first be necessary to establish good relations with the men, and that the best way of doing this might be to start a joint literacy campaign for both men and women.

As soon as this plan became known there was no lack of would-be students, but teachers were harder to find since the medium of instruction had to be English, faced with so many different vernaculars. With the consent of the Missions, school teachers were recruited and paid a small honorarium for taking two or three classes a week in their villages after school hours, and six full time paid supervisors were appointed to travel round the classes checking the attendances, coaching the teachers where necessary, and taking text books with them for sale, an essential part of the campaign since there was no bookshop in the area. Text books originally written for Ghana were used. They gave much practical information and taught the student how to cope with the modern world which was developing around him, but they had the disadvantage that they used Ghanian place names with which Cameroonians were not familiar and, had money permitted, a local edition would have been desirable. Nevertheless results were good and by the end of the course, which lasted for eighteen months to two years according to the regularity with which the classes met, a student who had presevered to the end could read and write about 1,500 words of English, do simple sums and could carry on by himself. About equal proportions of men and women attended, and a number of elderly Chiefs and Village Heads, some in their eighties. They were too old to make much progress but at least succeeded in learning to write their names thus removing a previous source of humiliation to them—the need to put their thumb prints on official documents.

Visiting the classes, mostly on foot, gave an opportunity to get to know the people and their background, and to become known. In one village a man teacher called Boniface was outstanding. Unusually he regarded the training he had had not as a bonus for himself but as something which fitted him to help the community, and his village, which was about five miles outside Kumbo, was also extremely progressive and eager to help itself. When the time was ripe therefore to begin to do something specifically for the women, Boniface was an obvious choice for the first organiser and his village, Kimar, for the first experiment.

XVI The corn mill societies

It took some years to establish the literacy campaign on a sound basis but, as it was something which was regarded by the people merely as an extension of the school programme with which they were already familiar, it was easily assimilated and proved an excellent means of preparing them for the more radical changes which were introduced later. These principally concerned the women. Whilst the men were by no means as idle as casual observers often thought, the chief burden of supporting the family was undoubtedly borne by the women. A man's cash-raising activities were normally confined to a few weeks of the year, but the women toiled unceasingly, market day affording their only break.

It was clear, therefore, that any attempt to help them must first begin by analysing their working methods to see in what way their labours could be reduced and, as has been mentioned earlier, an obvious hardship was the work involved in grinding their maize into flour. This they did between two stones, a large flat one on which the corn was scattered and a smaller stone, held in the hand, which was rubbed backwards and forwards over the surface of the larger stone. It could take an hour or more of monotonous work to produce even a small quantity of the flour and the women's hands were often covered with callouses. Dr Kaberry, in her book, had already suggested that corn mills might solve this problem and an opportune grant of £200 from the Nigerian Ministry of Education made it possible to set up a revolving loan fund to purchase ten mills when some could be found. There were none on sale in the Cameroons but they were eventually traced to a manufacturer in England. These mills, the design of which dated back to the middle of last century, were of cast iron and therefore somewhat unwieldy when it came to transporting them, especially the large wheel, but they were virtually unbreakable and required very little maintenance except for occasional oiling and the tightening up of nuts which had worked loose, and after a year or two the grinding plates needed changing—a quite simple operation. The bigger mills cost £20 each. A smaller model was not robust enough to stand up to the almost continuous use. Whilst this sum was not beyond the powers of the women to raise collectively, it was too much for most individuals to find, which meant that the societies had something attractive to offer members which they could not otherwise obtain. The mills therefore had a dual purpose they lightened the labours of the women but they also acted as "bait" to attract members to the societies.

Boniface was appointed the first paid corn mill organiser and the first mill was therefore taken to his village, Kimar. He was a man who had travelled quite a lot and had seen the mills in use in Nigeria. He therefore knew what a help they could be to the women. Even so it took all his eloquence to persuade them to accept one as a gift—they were afraid of the unknown. Eventually, however, a very elderly woman much respected in the village came down in its favour and the women reluctantly agreed to a demonstration. The mill, which broke down into a number of separate parts for head loading, was carried to the village and installed in the centre. Maize was poured down the funnel and two women very fearfully took the handles on either side and pushed. It would be nice to report that a steady stream of flour then emerged. In fact nothing happened at all, but trial and error eventually disclosed that new maize—as this was—must first be dried over a fire if it is not to stick between the grinding plates. Once this was done all was well, but the two women who had been turning the handles had not yet caught the necessary rhythm and had been using six times

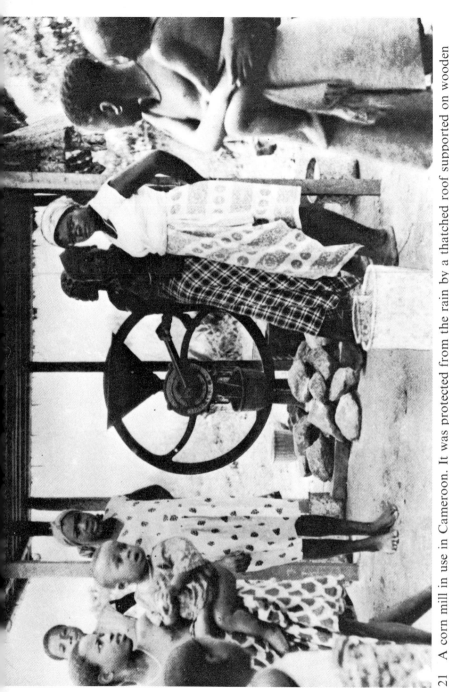

21 A corn mill in use in Cameroon. It was protected from the rain by a thatched roof supported on wooden posts. This mill was bolted to two wooden beams which were held down by large stones to prevent it from shifting. The mill was operated by two women but only one handle can be seen in this picture. The second handle was attached to the wheel.

the energy required pushing against each other. They now declared that it was too much hard work and the demonstration petered out. In a few days' time however, the situation had changed, the bolder spirits had become more familiar with the machine and it was soon in constant use, surviving the illness of an old lady and the claims of a witch doctor that this was due to these newfangled ideas.

The women's boasts of its prowess coupled with rural curiosity soon began to bring in sightseers from all over the area and very soon there were requests from other villages to set up corn mill societies there. The members of these societies were expected to pay for their machines, but were given a year in which to raise the money. At first they made a charge every time a woman used the mill but later it was found to be administratively simpler to charge a fixed sum a head each month. By the end of a year thirty villages had repaid their loans and more mills had been purchased and given out. The Fon's wives also received one for their own use since by custom they could not mix with the other women and, when the palace was burned down, they risked their lives to save it, the only thing in fact which was saved.

As the fame of the societies spread requests came in from other tribes and other organisers had to be appointed until eventually there were six of them covering the whole province. In a women's organisation it may seem strange that the staff were men, but the work involved much travelling on foot or bicycle and many nights away from home, and carrying the money received for repayments, they always ran the risk of attack. Most of them performed their duties admirably and were genuinely concerned to help the women. The reports that they brought back with them from the villages were an invaluable source of information as to what was going on in the province.

With a largely illiterate membership the rules for the societies had to be kept as simple as possible, the chief ones being that membership was open to any women regardless of tribe or religion and that the movement was non-political. The average membership was 70 members to a society, above a hundred was not encouraged as it was too many for the capacity of the machine and quarrels broke out as to whose turn it was to use it. Each society chose two head-women who held the key of the hut in which the mills were kept and, even though they were illiterate, they knew very well who had paid and who had not and seldom failed to have the money ready for the organisers when they called.

As the societies became established and the women had more leisure, the women's thoughts began to turn to other matters. They mostly live in family compounds rather than closely knit villages and until the societies were started many women met few people outside their own family, except perhaps on market day. The corn mills changed all that, and just as in England in the old days women could always be found gossiping round the village pump, so anyone visiting the area could be sure of finding some women waiting their turn to use the mill. From this the idea developed that the members should have regularly monthly meetings and, after these had been running for a few months, they began to feel the need to do something useful at them and asked for classes in such subjects as soapmaking and cookery. There were not enough trained domestic science teachers available, however, to make it possible to send them to each village and so, instead, the classes were held in a central village to which the members walked in, ten or twelve neighbouring villages being grouped together for this purpose.

These measures, however, were only satisfactory in the dry season, when the classes could be held outside. In the rains it was necessary to have some sort of meeting house and so the women, with the same gift for organisation which had been shown when the Fon's palace was burnt down, set about building community halls for the classes. They made the bricks, carried in the bamboos and bullied their husbands into doing the bricklaying and carpentering. Each group vied with the others. Kimar, which built the first hall, pulled it down two years later as it was not large enough for the hundred or more women who used to turn up to the classes from all over the district. One group, lacking a good leader, ran into difficulties and its hall remained in an un-

112

22 (a) Men and women from a number of villages in the Cameroons assembled to discuss the meeting hall which can be seen, not yet finished, on the extreme left. The women made the bricks and donated the bamboos for the roof which are lying in the foreground, and the men did the actual bricklaying. (b) The hall almost completed. When this picture was taken, the walls had still to be plastered. The cost of this building was borne by the people themselves.

finished state for several months until the other groups, entirely of their own volition, came to its rescue by offering money and labour to complete it, an unheard of gesture at the time since concern for one's neighbour, until then, had stopped at the family.

These halls also benefited the villages in which they were built as the Medical Department came to use them for monthly clinics which, until then, had been few and far between.

Gradually the range of subjects was extended to include child welfare and hygiene. These were followed up by one week residential courses in the school holidays when a girls' school was hired and two women from each of twenty villages were brought in. Possessing the excellent memories of illiterates the women had no difficulty in memorising what they had been taught and in passing this on to their fellow members on their return home. As they began to put into practice what they had learnt, a marked improvement could be seen in their health and that of their children. With *foo foo* more freely available they put on weight and far fewer babies died of malnutrition. Their husbands also prospered, and once they realised how much they themselves benefited from what the women were doing they became active supporters of the societies and no longer objected to their wives leaving home to attend meetings. Some even asked, quite seriously whether similar societies might not be started for them!

XVII Projects carried out by the societies

Whilst the societies, after some four years, were now firmly established and enquiries were being received from tribes living down at the coast, various problems were beginning to arise. One minor one was that they had been formed on the basis of the collective ownership of the corn mill. Many women, who for one reason or another had not joined when the society was started in their village, now wished to do so and the founder members objected on the grounds that they had not contributed anything towards the cost of the mill. After much discussion this was overcome by issuing these newcomers with red badges (the original ones were yellow) signifying that, whilst they might take part in all the other activities, they were not entitled to use the mill. The women were extremely proud of their membership and very old women often used to enquire anxiously whether their daughters might inherit their place in the society after their death.

Another difficulty which arose occasionally was attempts to confine membership of a society to a restricted group of women, for example those belonging to a Mission, but this was easily overcome by refusing to provide a corn mill until there was evidence that all the women in the village had been given the opportunity of joining if they wished to do so. Because of this the corn mill societies were perhaps the only group in the country which could claim members from every section of the community and from every tribe and religious denomination.

About this time (1956) a more serious setback occurred in the Nsaw area. An unsuccessful attempt was made to dethrone the Fon, fighting broke out, a number of villages were burnt down and a large body of police from Nigeria had to be quartered in Kumbo for several weeks (normally there were none, and the Fon maintained order through his own police). Great care had to be taken at this time not to be associated in the Fon's mind with the opposition party, the leader of which had been banished by the Administration, and for a time it became wiser to concentrate on areas outside Nsaw. Eventually, however, the bad feeling died down and the societies resumed their activities.

Trouble also broke out about the same time, but for different reasons, in the Wum area. The societies had not yet been started there, as it was some 150 miles by road from Kumbo, but, when a particular group of women (politically inspired) started terrorising the other women by destroying their farms and beating them up, and the military had to be brought in, the Administration asked that an attempt should be made to introduce the societies there too. This was done, beginning on the perimeter of the troubled area and gradually working inwards. As the mills could not be purchased locally, possession of them was a highly effective bargaining counter. Most villages were eager to possess them and it was possible therefore to build up a body of women who acted both as a stabilising influence and a protection for each other, so that the power of the other group was eventually broken. The troubles left an unpleasant aftermath for some years, however, since witchcraft and ju ju had all been invoked by the ring leaders.

Elsewhere in the Province there were now ten groups, totalling between them over 200 individual societies with a membership altogether of some 18,000 women. These groups, each of which elected their own leaders, just as the societies did, now turned their attention to other problems, one of the most serious being the damage done to their farms by straying cattle, belonging to the Fulani and by the horses, sheep and goats more often belonging to the local people. In the past, although they had the right of complaint to the

116

District Officers, the women were usually at a disadvantage when it came to stating their case. They were a poor match for the more sophisticated Fulani or the Village Heads who were mostly the owners of the offending sheep and goats. They rambled on, repeated themselves, and exaggerated their claims so wildly that the District Officer understandably lost patience with them. The same thing happened in the Native Courts, where they stood little chance against their wealthier and more influential opponents. Properly organised however and able to put their complaints collectively the situation began to change, the Fulani increasingly began to be fined for cattle offences which they had previously been able to get away with, and the situation improved still more when the women decided that it was time to fence the farming areas in.

This solution, which seems simple, was in fact revolutionary and presented many difficulties. Land ownership is always an explosive subject in Africa and one which the Administration was reluctant to tackle. The consent of all the villages affected had first to be obtained and the exact line of the cattle boundary determined, no easy task in a country still without maps. Stone markers existed but they had quite often been moved—by both sides. After these hurdles had been surmounted, the fencing posts had to be cut and money raised to buy the barbed wire. Like the corn mills this had to be imported and the weight of the rolls, designed for lorry transport, created difficulties when it came to carrying them since many miles of wire was required. A less ambitious plan might have been to have fenced in the sheep and goats instead and to have forced the Fulani to employ the herdsmen that the law, in fact, required them to do, but the animals might well have died from starvation and thirst as they were usually left to fend for themselves, so the women enclosed their farming land instead. There were problems, of course. At first, the Fulani drove their cattle against the fences in an attempt to trample them down and sometimes succeeded and white ants ate the posts away but, in the end, the two pilot schemes carried out proved a success and other areas began to follow suit. As with the mills the society members bore the whole cost themselves and provided all the necessary labour free, but they were given time in which to repay the loans given to them to buy the wire.

The necessity to raise this money directly affected the agricultural programme in the province since the women put more land under cultivation in order to have surplus food to sell in the markets. Moreover, societies often started a society farm, the proceeds for which went into the society's funds. The farms were farmed collectively and proved very useful when it was desired to carry out some experiment which the women would have been reluctant to risk on their own farms for fear of failure.

The policy of the Agricultural Department, for a number of years, had been actively to discourage women from farming at all and to try to persuade the men to take their place— with a conspicuous lack of success. As the influence of the societies gradually made itself felt, however, the Department began to appreciate that they were far more open to new ideas than the men and far harder working so that, when the groups were set up, agricultural assistants were appointed to work with the dozen or more villages which belonged to each of them. In this way, for the first time, the women began to be taught better farming techniques. They began to understand the need for contour farming and a few of the more enterprising were persuaded to plant new strains of corn. When their harvest proved exceptionally good, the other women followed them. Soon enough corn was grown to carry the women right through the year and the period when they had to "make do" with potatoes was a thing of the past.

This surplus however brought storage problems, owing to the improved standards of housing. In the older type of mud hut the grain was stored in the loft where the smoke from the cooking fire below helped to keep weevils and other pests away. Now that mud brick buildings with zinc roofs were becoming more common, this necessitated outside kitchens, the old method of storage was no longer effective and, unsmoked, a great deal of the surplus was destroyed. A

number of experiments were carried out to find ways of
overcoming the problem, and it was found that one of the
best methods was to pack the corn in old four gallon
kerosene tins, which were then sealed and the air pumped
out creating a vacuum in which the pests could not live.

Poultry schemes were also started, the bran from the
milled corn being used to feed the chickens. Nearly every
compound had a few hens scratching round but they were of
very poor stock and the eggs they produced were so small
that, when cooking, three had to be used where the recipe
called for one. The gift of a few Rhode Island Reds helped
to change this and with cross breeding the local stock
improved.

Fuel plantations were another project that the members
tackled. Firewood was very scarce in some areas but the
Forest Department, when it endeavoured to improve the
situation by planting eucalyptus trees, usually had great
difficulty in acquiring the land. All requests of this nature
from the Administration were usually regarded with deep
suspicion, but the landowners were much more willing to
negotiate with their fellow villagers. Soon a number of plots
had been acquired for this purpose, the Department providing the seedlings and the women the labour. By planting a
stand of eucalyptus every year for seven years, after the
initial period of waiting for the trees to grow, a steady
supply of firewood was ensured for the foreseeable future,
since the trees began to grow again as soon as they had been
cut down providing their roots were not damaged.

Although the province was well watered and there were
numerous streams cascading down the hillsides, water was
still a problem for most of the villages. It had to be fetched
from the stream, which in the dry season might be only a
trickle, and it was often polluted by animals and by people
bathing in it. In some areas a small muddy pool of semi-
stagnant water was all that was available for perhaps two
or three hundred people. The societies therefore started a
number of schemes to provide small storage tanks into which
the water was led from the nearest stream or spring, the
overflow from the tank providing overhead showers and

supplying a small wash house. Instead of standing up to their knees in the often icy water the women could wash their clothes in comfort, the roof affording them much needed shade during the dry season.

Finally the women embarked on their most ambitious scheme, a shop run on co-operative principles. Most of their household purchases were made in the market. Cash payments were rare, and the women usually bartered their produce for whatever they required. Increasingly, however, locally made articles such as the clay pots they used for cooking and for carrying water were giving way to Western goods made of cast iron or enamel and, later of plastic. Whilst aesthetically this was a pity it had to be admitted that the old type of pot broke very easily and, if the Western substitute cost twice as much, it lasted at least four times as long. Unfortunately whilst the women were shrewd bargainers in the case of things to which they were accustomed, they were out of their depth when it came to buying these unfamiliar goods and were often tricked by the traders into paying absurd prices for poor quality articles. In addition many of the things they now felt a need for, such as better types of farming implements, sewing machines and barbed wire, were not sold at all in the market and so an old building in Kumbo was converted into a store and five thousand women each subscribed two shillings for shares in it. With this capital and a good deal of extended credit from the wholesalers at the coast, the shop was stocked with general hardware, text books for the literacy classes and anything else not readily obtainable locally. Care was taken, however, not to conflict with the market traders by selling such items as Manchester cottons and soap and, probably for this reason, very little opposition was encountered from them.

Although they had a very clear idea of what they wanted, the committee formed to run the shop was not yet capable of actually managing it. The book keeping was beyond them and so a retired school teacher was appointed for this purpose, but the women took every opportunity of making it clear to him that they were in charge! By midday, on the opening day, the entire stock was sold out as several

120

thousand women converged upon the shop from all directions but, as the novelty wore off, the sales became less spectacular and settled down to a steady but not dramatic weekly income since prices, which were fixed, were kept as low as possible. Soon plans were laid for a second shop thirty miles away, and the Co-operative Department, which until then had confined its activities to men, began to take an interest and is now supervising several stores.

XVIII Envoi

Times were changing however. Whereas the Chiefs and government officials formerly went everywhere on foot or horseback, travelling in short stages, sleeping in the villages and mixing freely with the people, they now rode round in cars. They began to lose touch with their people and no longer knew what they were thinking or doing. In the past the District Officer's standard of living had differed very little from that of the people whom he was administering. Whilst there were no motor roads he too had to be content with oil lamps and live on what could be obtained locally. Now lorries brought in transistor radio sets, portable lighting plants, electric fans and refrigerators which he and the Chiefs could afford, but the poorer people could not although they now knew that such things existed and coveted them. The gap between the "haves" and the "have nots" noticeably widened and discontent increased.

Meanwhile, with talk of independence in the air, the politicians and their parties proliferated and the power which was formerly in the hands of the Chiefs was gradually transferred to them. In 1960 the British Government decided that the country was too small to be economically viable by itself and that in order to achieve independence the people must either join with Nigeria or with the part of the Cameroons formerly administered by France. A plebiscite was held, under United Nations supervision, to decide the issue. Feelings ran high, and as the largest organised body in the country the corn mill societies were under repeated pressure to join one or the other of the two main political parties, and constant vigilance was necessary to ensure that their neutrality was not infringed. All that could be done in such a situation was to see that the women had equal opportunity with the men to attend the explanatory meetings held by the Plebiscite Officials so that they at least understood for what they were voting.

One of the greatest achievements of the societies over the years had been the gradual breaking down of the barriers between tribes so that the women worked amicably with each other regardless of their different origins. In Africa the family comes first, the tribe next and the country a very poor third. Now tribal feeling was deliberately built up again by the politicians and organisers living outside their own tribal areas began to fear for their safety. In the atmosphere of distrust and suspicion which developed, people no longer went out after dark or wandered far from their homes and the opportunity was taken by some to settle old scores. In particular Boniface came in for rough handling from people who had been successfully prosecuted for cattle trespass as the result of his investigations of the women's complaints, and it was difficult to afford him protection. He was now Senior Corn Mill Organiser and the success of the societies owed a great deal to his untiring efforts on their behalf.

Throughout this unrest the women remained an influence for good in the community but they were powerless to control events. When the result of the plebiscite proved to be a decision to become a part of the Federal Republic of Cameroun, the British Officials were withdrawn and a number of junior staff asked for transfer, those of Nigerian origin leaving the country altogether. Others, including Boniface, were deservedly promoted and went down to the coast. This left gaps which it was impossible to fill as there were not enough trained personnel left to go round. The societies continued but for some time they were left very much to their own devices without teachers for their classes or agricultural assistants to help them with their farming programmes. It is a tribute to the ability of their leaders that they survived this period of neglect and change. It is good to be able to report, however, that trained Community Development organisers are once more working with them whilst the improvements they sponsored and carried out, which have been described in these pages, have made a lasting contribution to their well-being and that of the community in general. The women have effectively demonstrated their ability and willingness to help themselves and others and they will never return to their former poverty and ignorance.

Appendix
Some international organisations connected with overseas aid

The following list of some of the organisations concerned with overseas aid may be of help to the reader. Organisations which are indented are controlled by the organisation immediately preceding them, although they have separate offices.

THE UNITED NATIONS ORGANISATION
1 U.N. Economic and Social Council (ECOSOC)
   United Nations
   New York N.Y. 10017
   United States of America
   2 Economic Commission for Africa
      P.O. Box 3001
      Addis Ababa
      Ethiopia
   3 Economic Commission for Asia and the Far East
      Sala Santitham, Rajadamnern Avenue
      Bangkok
      Thailand
   4 Economic Commission for Europe
      Palais des Nations
      1211 Geneva 22
      Switzerland
   5 Economic Commission for Latin America
      Avenida Dag Hammarskjold
      Santiago
      Chile

6   Office of the High Commissioner for Refugees
Palais des Nations
1211 Geneva 22
Switzerland

7   U.N. Relief and Works Agency for Palestine
Refugees (UNRWA)
Museitbeh Quarter,
Beirut,
Lebanon

8   International Labour Organisation (ILO)
CH 1211 Geneva 22
Switzerland

9   Food and Agricultural Organisation (FAO)
Viale delle Terme di Carcalla
00100 Rome
Italy

10   World Food Program
Viale delle Terme di Caracalla
00100 Rome
Italy

11   U.N. Educational, Scientific and Cultural Organisation
(UNESCO)
Place de Fontenoy
75 Paris 7e
France

12   Co-ordinating Committee for International
Voluntary Service
UNESCO HOUSE, 1, rue Miollis
75 Paris 15e
France

13   World Health Organisation (WHO)
1211 Geneva 27
Switzerland

14   International Bank for Reconstruction and
Development
1818 H. Street N.W.
Washington D.C. 20433
United States of America

15 International Monetary Fund (IMF)
19th and H. Streets N.W.
Washington D.C. 20431
United States of America

16 International Finance Corporation (IFC)
1818 H. Street N.W.
Washington D.C. 20433
United States of America

17 International Development Association (IDA)
1818 H. Street N.W.
Washington D.C. 20433
United States of America

18 U.N. Childrens' Fund (UNICEF)
United Nations,
New York, N.Y. 10017
United States of America

19 U.N. Development Programme (UNDP)
United Nations
New York N.Y. 10017
United States of America

20 U.N. Conference on Trade and Development
Palais des Nations
1211 Geneva 10
Switzerland

21 U.N. Research Institute for Social Development
Palais des Nations
1211 Geneva 10
Switzerland

22 U.N. Institute for Training and Research
801 United Nations Plaza
New York
United States of America

INTER-GOVERNMENTAL ORGANISATIONS

23 Afro–Asian Rural Reconstruction Organisation
C/117–118 Defence Colony
New Delhi 3
India

Aid and self-help

24 Asian and Pacific Council
   Economic Department, Ministry of Foreign Affairs
   Saranrom Palace
   Bangkok
   Thailand
25 African Development Bank
   B.P. No. 1387
   Abidjan
   Ivory Coast
26 Asian Development Bank
   P.O. Box 126
   Makati
   Rizal
   Philippines
27 Association of S.E. Asian Nations
   14 Merdeka Barat
   Djakarta
   Indonesia
28 Caribbean Food and Nutrition Institute
   University of the West Indies,
   Mona
   Kingston 7
   Jamaica
29 Colombo Plan Council for Technical Co-operation in
   S. and S.E. Asia
   B.P. 596
   Colombo
   Ceylon
30 Commonwealth Agricultural Bureaux
   Farnham House
   Farnham Royal, Bucks.
   England
31 East African Community
   P.O. Box 1001
   Arusha
   Tanzania

32 Institute of Nutrition of Central American and Panama
Carretera Roosevelt, Zona 11
Aptdo. Postal 11–88
Guatemala

33 Inter-American Committee for Agricultural Development
1735 Eye Street N.W.
Washington D.C.
United States of America

34 International Relief Union
12 Chemin de Malombre,
Geneva
Switzerland

35 International Rice Commission
FAO Regional Office
Maliwan Mansions
Phra Atit Road
Bangkok
Thailand

36 International Secretariat for Volunteer Service
12 Chemin de Surville
1213 Geneva
Switzerland

37 League of Arab States
Midan Al Tahrir
Cairo
United Arab Republic

38 Organisation of African Unity
P.O. Box 3243
Addis Ababa
Ethiopia

39 Organisation of American States
Pan American Union,
Washington D.C. 20006
United States of America

40   Organisation for Economic Co-operation and Development
      Chateau de la Muette
      2 rue Andre Pascal
      75 Paris 16e
      France
41   South East Asia Treaty Organisation
      Sri Ayudhaya Road
      P.O. Box 517
      Bangkok
      Thailand
42   South Pacific Commission
      Anse Vata
      Noumea (P.B.9)
      New Caledonia
43   Union of Central African States
      B.P. 873
      Bangui
      Republique Centrafricaine

INTERNATIONAL NON-GOVERNMENTAL ORGANISATIONS HAVING CONSULTATIVE STATUS WITH THE UNITED NATIONS ORGANISATION
44   Afro–Asian Organisation for Economic Organisation
      Cairo Chamber of Commerce Building,
      Midan Al-Falaki
      Cairo
      United Arab Republic
45   Associated Country Women of the World
      50/51 Warwick Square
      London S.W.1
      England
46   Association for the Study of World Refugee Problems
      P.O. Box 34 706
      Vaduz
      Liechtenstein

47 Caritas Internationalis
    Piazza S. Calisto 16
    00153 Rome
    Italy
48 Conference of African Women
    B.P. 370
    Bamako
    Mali
49 Co-operative for American Relief Everywhere (CARE)
    660 First Avenue
    New York N.Y. 10016
    United States of America
50 Federation of Asian Women's Associations
    Escoda Memorial Building
    1501 San Marcelino Street
    Ermita
    Manilla
    Philippines
51 International Catholic Rural Association
    Via XXIV Maggio 43
    00187 Rome
    Italy
52 International Co-operation for Socio-Economic
    Development
    51–61 Avenue Adolphe Lacomble
    1040 Brussels
    Belgium
53 International Committee of the Red Cross
    7 Avenue de la Paix
    1211 Geneva 1
    Switzerland
54 International Co-operative Alliance
    11 Upper Grosvenor Street
    London W1X 9PA
    England
55 International Council of Voluntary Agencies
    7 Avenue de la Paix
    1211 Geneva
    Switzerland

56 International Council of Women
    13 rue Caumartin
    75 Paris 9e
    France
57 International Federation of Home Economics
    64 avenue Edouard Vaillant
    92 Boulogne
    France
58 International Planned Parenthood Federation
    18–20 Lower Regent Street
    London S.W.1
    England
59 International Social Service
    58 rue du Stand
    1211 Geneva 11
    Switzerland
60 International Union for Health Education
    20 rue Greuze
    75 Paris 16e
    France
61 International Voluntary Service
    Gartenhofstrasse 7
    8004 Zurich
    Switzerland
62 International Council on Social Welfare
    345 East 46th Street
    New York N.Y. 10017
    United States of America
63 League of Red Cross Societies
    17 Chemin des Crêts
    Petit–Saconnex
    1211 Geneva 19
    Switzerland
64 Lutheran World Federation (Dept of World Service)
    150 Route de Ferney
    1211 Geneva 20
    Switzerland

65   Pan Pacific and S.E. Asia Women's Association
     Secretary, Mrs Dodson, 9 Courtville Flats,
     Parliament Street
     Auckland 1
     New Zealand
66   World Association for the Struggle Against Hunger
     Centre International,
     Place des Nations
     1–3 Varembé
     1202 Geneva
     Switzerland
67   The Salvation Army
     101 Queen Victoria Street
     P.O. Box 249
     London E.C.4
     England
68   World Muslim Congress
     171B Block 3
     PECHS
     Karachi 29
     Pakistan

OTHER INTERNATIONAL ORGANISATIONS
DEALING WITH DEVELOPING COUNTRIES
69   Africa Co-operative Savings and Credit Association
     Silopark House
     P.O. Box 3278
     Nairobi
     Kenya
70   African Adult Education Association
     Prof. Lalage Bown
     University of Zambia
     P.O. Box 2379
     Lusaka
     Zambia

71 Afro–Asian Housing Association
P.O. Box 523
28 Ramses Street
Cairo
United Arab Republic

72 American Council of Voluntary Agencies for Foreign Service Inc.
200 Park Avenue South
New York N.Y. 10003
United States of America

73 Association of Social Work Education in Africa
The School of Social Work
Haile Selassie I University
P.O. Box 1176, Addis Ababa
Ethiopia

74 Catholic Relief Services
350 Fifth Avenue
New York N.Y. 10001
United States of America

75 Church World Service
475 Riverside Drive
New York N.Y. 10027
United States of America

76 Community Development Foundation Inc.
345 East 46th Street
New York N.Y. 10017
United States of America

77 Foundation for the peoples of the South Pacific
125 West 55th Street
New York N.Y. 10019
United States of America

78 German Bishops' Relief Fund (MISEREOR)
P.O. Box 1450
Mozartstrasse 11
Aachen
Federal Republic of Germany

79 Intermediate Technology Development Group Ltd.
9 King Street
London W.C.2
England
80 International Council on Social Welfare
345 East 46th Street
New York N.Y. 10017
United States of America
81 International Institute of Rural Development
IIRR Manila Office, Elena Apts
512 Romero Sales Street,
Ermila
Manila
Philippines
82 International Organisation for Rural Development
20 rue du Commerce
1040 Brussels
Belgium
83 International Rice Research Institute
Los Baños
Laguna
Philippines
84 International Society for Community Development
345 East 46th Street
New York N.Y. 100!7
United States of America
85 Oxfam
274 Banbury Road
Oxford OX2 7DZ
England
86 Pan-American Institute for Development
1 rue de Varembé
1202 Geneva
Switzerland
87 Pan American Health Organisation
525 23rd Street N.W.
Washington D.C. 20037
United States of America

88 Pan American Development Foundation
19 and Constitution Avenue N.W.
Washington D.C. 20006
United States of America

89 Save the Children Fund
29 Queen Anne's Gate
London S.W.1
England

90 Society for International Development
1346 Connecticut Avenue N.W.
Washington D.C. 20036
United States of America

91 Technoserve Inc.
P.O. Box 90, Greenwich
Connecticut 06830
United States of America

92 Vienna Institute for Development
Obere Donaustrasse 49–51
A 1020 Vienna
Austria

93 Voluntary and Christian Service (Help the Aged)
8–10 Denman Street,
London W1A 2AP
England

94 Voluntary Committee on Overseas Aid and Development
69 Victoria Street
London S.W.1
England

95 Voluntary Service Overseas
3 Hanover Street
London W.1
England

96 War on Want
10 The Green
London W.5
England

97 World Council of Credit Unions
    1617 Sherman Avenue
    P.O. Box 431
    Madison
    Wisconsin 53701
    United States of America
98 World Fellowship of Buddhists
    41 Phra Atit Road
    Bangkok
    Thailand
99 World Neighbours
    5116 North Portland
    Oklahoma City
    Oklahoma 73112
100 World Council of Churches
    150 Route de Ferney
    1211 Geneva 20
    Switzerland

Index

139